**Pacific Standard Time: LA/LA**
Latin American & Latino Art in LA

Presenting Sponsors

 The Getty

Bank of America

From Latin America to Hollywood: Latino Film Culture in Los Angeles 1967-2017 is part of Pacific Standard Time: LA/LA, a far-reaching and ambitious exploration of Latin American and Latino art in dialogue with Los Angeles, taking place from September 2017 through January 2018 at more than 70 cultural institutions across Southern California. Pacific Standard Time is an initiative of the Getty. The presenting sponsor is Bank of America.

Major support for this program and publication is provided through grants from the Getty Foundation. *El Norte* (1983) was restored in 2017 by the Academy Film Archive, supported in part by the Getty Foundation.

 The Getty Foundation

This project was made possible with support from California Humanities, a non-profit partner of the National Endowment for the Humanities. Visit www.calhum.org.

Additional support is provided, in part, by the Los Angeles County Board of Supervisors through the Los Angeles County Arts Commission.

The Ballad of Gregorio Cortez (1982) was restored in 2016 by the Academy Film Archive. This project is supported in part by an award from the National Endowment for the Arts. To find out more about how National Endowment for the Arts grants impact individuals and communities, visit www.arts.gov.

 CALIFORNIA HUMANITIES   Los Angeles County Arts Commission   ART WORKS.   National Endowment for the Arts arts.gov

FROM LATIN AMERICA TO HOLLYWOOD: LATINO FILM CULTURE IN LOS ANGELES 1967-2017

Academy of Motion Picture Arts and Sciences

FOREWORD BY SANDRA CISNEROS

Academy Imprints

CONTENTS

FOREWORD

I grew up going to the movies in two languages. In Chicago, the Spanish-language theaters were as *apachurrados* as a pair of old *chanclas*, but the stories they told were shimmering in moon dust, the color, to this day, of my favorite films.

We tolerated feral herds of galloping children in the aisles and the howls of unhappy babies. Only gringos would be so barbaric as to leave their kids with strangers.

Never mind that Mother and I had to watch the film like geishas, with our legs tucked beneath our butts because of rats. Once the film began we forgot about the urban wildlife and found ourselves in a familiar and comforting world where people looked and talked like us.

Back then features opened with a Mexican newsreel that began and ended with Picasso's *Don Quijote* accompanied by an extra-loud military band playing "Jesusita in Chihuahua," a tune from the Mexican Revolution. This alerted everyone buying their pumpkin seeds and *tortas* at the candy counter to hurry to their seat.

Why did the films always begin with the same problem? An annoying hair quivering on the projector lens till our angry whistles jolted the projectionist from his nap.

On screen, we traveled across an invented Mexican landscape crowned with magueys and canopied with dramatic clouds. *Charros* on horseback serenaded *señoritas* on balconies, and everybody sang.

Or maybe the story was set in a romantic nightclub with Toña la Negra murmuring an Agustín Lara hit in her rum-and-Coca-Cola voice.

Or the story was about a humble *vecindad* and its lovable inhabitants. Pedro Infante was a hunk even as a poor but noble carpenter. Millions of foolish girls like me dreamed we would one day marry him even though he had died in a plane crash when I was a toddler.

At my grandparents' house in Mexico City our Saturday afternoons were spent at the movie house named for our neighborhood, el Tepeyac, a theater so mine-shaft-dark, you had to light a match to find a seat. The bonus of watching a film at el Tepeyac was the ad-libbed dialogue from the audience, always more entertaining than the script.

El Tepeyac may have been just a flea-infested dump, but we loved it. After the matinee, everyone poured out into the bright sunshine and walked together in the street, a spontaneous parade of people who had experienced something wonderful.

In the States the movies I saw in English were wide-screen epics in cartoon technicolor. They inspired me to create elaborate sets for my Barbie dolls with library books and chiffon scarves after witnessing a sexually-frustrated Richard Burton tear a gauze bed curtain with a dagger just to get at Liz Cleopatra.

Movies in English told tales of an exotic world we watched like visitors from another planet, especially if the film was set in the United States. Going to the movies was a big deal for our family of nine, and we went often, even if we had to bring our own popcorn in a paper grocery bag. Poor Father, whose grasp of English was slippery, often lost the thread of the plot, and we had to whisper our translations.

"*¿Qué, qué, qué? ¿Qué dijo?*" Father asked us.

"Shhh!" a voice from behind us answered.

But it was heartbreaking to see our beloved Cantinflas wasted in *Around the World in 80 Days*, where he wasn't even the featured star. Luckily, we saw this snoozer in our pajamas at a drive-in.

I was in college when I first went to a movie alone. A girl terrified of everything, I convinced myself I'd be safe since this was a "film" screened at the respectable Art Institute of Chicago, right across the street from the gas company where I worked, not *un churro* at the Teatro Villa on Blue Island. After a day of arguing on the phone with customers, I crossed Michigan Avenue and found myself in a pristine auditorium where no one ate *tortas* or shouted back to the screen.

The film was Federico Fellini's *The White Sheik*, the story of a country girl in love with a character from a *fumetti,* a photo comic just like the Mexican *fotonovelas* Father and I read. I watched the film with my mouth open.

This Fellini film led me to his others. One, set in an Italian vaudeville theater during World War II, shows us the theater audience, a rowdy crowd that heckles the performers, talks to one another during the acts, gobbles submarine sandwiches, and even allows a toddler to pee in the aisle. It was just like the Mexican movie houses.

Fellini opened the door to other foreign movies that weren't so foreign, and I started attending Chicago film festivals and alternative movie houses, like Facets Multimedia on West Fullerton Avenue where I caught *El Super*, the story of an unhappy New York immigrant who dreams of going back home to Cuba.

I remember that film primarily for a party scene where the furniture has been cleared so everyone can dance. This crowded living room packed with Botero-esque bodies was not created in Hollywood or Churubusco, but from the imagination of an immigrant like us. I had never seen my home on the big screen before.

Since then I've recognized myself in the stories told by many other Latin American filmmakers, especially those written by Latinas, like María Novaro's *Danzón* and Patricia Cardoso's adaptation of Josefina López's *Real Women Have Curves*, two films where real women have sex and don't die as a result.

Remember the monster films of the 1950s? My Grandpa Cordero would spit, "*¡Puro Drácula!*" when he found anything to be absolutely unbelievable. How were we to know we would become the monsters after the fall of the Twin Towers on 9/11?

Puro Drácula. What story do we tell now as Latino storytellers? What can we create that is beyond what history has invented for us? What will the codices of our time—film—depict to tell us where we are going?

SANDRA CISNEROS
June 28th, 2017, Casa Coatlicue, San Miguel de Allende

INTRODUCTION

Southern California has long been more of a northern outpost of Latin America than a land apart, sharing a history of fluid borders and porous interchange between them, both on literal maps and across the boundaries of their ever-changing societies. Two centuries after Spaniards first encountered indigenous residents, the city of Los Angeles was named "El Pueblo de Nuestra Señora la Reina de los Ángeles del Río Porciúncula" in 1781 by founders who were already a robust mix of indigenous, European and African ancestry. New borderlines appeared after 1848. Manifest Destiny fueled a US invasion of Mexico, leading to Mexico ceding half of its territory, including California.

The border and the growth of white American society in Los Angeles could not extinguish the region's deeply enmeshed cultures and the interpersonal stories that are shared among the inhabitants of the vast, continuous stretch of land between L.A. and Latin America. But it contributed to the growth of simultaneous sensations of belonging, otherness, inclusion, and alienation, which co-exist within the inhabitants themselves; as the band Los Tigres del Norte sing in *Somos Más Americanos*, "I didn't cross the border, the border crossed me."

When, in 2014, the Getty announced that the next incarnation of its established "Pacific Standard Time" exhibition grant programs would focus on the intersection between the arts and cultures of Los Angeles and Latin America, it seemed the perfect opportunity to explore this interplay in the realm of filmmaking. With Hollywood as the global commercial 'capital' of the movie industry since its early decades, and the significant impact made in this art form by filmmakers of Latin American heritage, the Academy of Motion Picture Arts and Sciences set out to define a project that could begin to examine this dynamic. Our time frame, 1967-2017, was historically significant in Latin America. In response to rising political repression in several countries, Latin American cinema developed an audacious voice of its own. Film directors consciously forged a dynamic and inventive body of work that reflected their reality. While Los Angeles is part of Latin America, ironically Latinos living here were marginalized and unable to fully develop a significant cinematic representation in proportion to their presence in this region.

This publication is one component among many being presented as part of *From Latin America to Hollywood: Latino Film Culture in Los Angeles 1967*-2017. It is the result of a complex four-year odyssey to document, in their own voices, the stories of Latino and Latin American filmmakers, and to understand their relationship with filmic "Los Angeles" in its many incarnations—the motion picture 'industry,' independent film and the festival experience, the social impact of movies and their critical reception, and their part in creating this mythology of "Hollywood."

How could we harness the many moving parts of a large film organization and create a compelling project that would contribute to the archival record of film history, and create a template for further recognition of these important but historically underrepresented filmmakers? We elected to anchor the project in the Academy's already successful Oral History Project, for which over

150 deeply researched filmed interviews have thus far been conducted, and to use the films of the participating filmmakers as inspiration for the subsequent screening series, film restorations, collections acquisitions, education programs, project website, and publication.

The topic is so vast that we could easily have thrown up our hands at the enormity—and the impossibility—of accurately covering fifty years of Latino and Latin American filmmaking, its impact globally, and its reach across the more than half-dozen countries represented. We immediately recognized the need to acknowledge this project as the start of a deeper commitment to continuing this work long after the *Pacific Standard Time: LA/LA* exhibitions have been presented in Southern California between September of 2017 and January of 2018.

The in-depth, on-camera Visual History Interviews were conducted over 2 ½ years, across three continents, and in three languages. The thirteen filmmakers we interviewed, selected with input from our Advisory Committee, include directors, writers, and producers, and represent a range of generations, creative origins, filmmaking styles and genres, political orientations, countries, and a relative balance of genders. Our 'wish list' was of course far longer, and some of the completed interviews are the result of good luck and timing, while other subjects still on our list await future Academy Visual History tapings.

We interviewed legends, rising stars, iconoclasts, and those who deserved more expansive careers than their era may have allowed. We spoke with filmmakers who work in their language or country of origin, and those who have crossed borders, cultures, and adopted different languages to make their films. The resultant 42 hours of videotaped first-person interviews form the core primary source materials from which the eight authors in this publication drew their research and inspiration. In addition, the Academy Oral History Projects department used the opportunities presented by filming trips to Mexico, Brazil, France, and other locations, both international and within the United States, to film additional related interviews—at the time of publication, an additional thirteen of these Visual Histories have been recorded, and new subjects will continue to be added over time. This footage will be progressively released on the project's website, with rich metadata that allows in-depth exploration and the ability to search across themes, exploring linkages among artists from diverse backgrounds, all speaking the universal language of storytelling.

This publication too will live online, as will the public programming content for the Academy's screening series and in-person celebrations of these filmmakers, which will include the presentation of several new film restorations by the Academy Film Archive and other cultural partners. We see the collaborations this project has engendered—between researchers, authors, archivists, and artists—as a metaphor for the ways in which borders can be approached across disciplines and between peoples. We celebrate our communal need to tell our stories and acknowledge the rich and complicated geographical, intellectual, and emotional terrain that we share.

LOS HISTORIAS QUE CONTARON

ORAL HISTORIES FROM 50 YEARS OF LATIN AMERICAN FILMMAKING

BY: LOURDES PORTILLO

PROLOGUE:
THE THINGS THEY CARRIED

I was delighted to be invited by the Academy of Motion Picture Arts and Sciences to be the guest curator for a film series of key works of Latin American cinema, the institution's contribution to the Getty initiative, *Pacific Standard Time: LA/LA*. The Academy's film component, *From Latin America to Hollywood: Latino Film Culture in Los Angeles 1967–2017*, gave me the opportunity not only to select seminal narrative films, but also to conduct oral history interviews with the films' directors, producers, and writers. As a Mexican-born filmmaker living

in the U.S. since adolescence, I had already met all the filmmakers except one. For the oral histories, I interviewed all but two of them in person. (Due to Brazilian travel logistics, I managed two oral histories long distance while an interlocutor conducted the interviews.)

Across the five-decade era covered by this project, Latin American cinema burst into life against a backdrop of repression, with authoritarian regimes in many Latin American countries, and outright dictatorships in others. A time of discontent and dissent, this period also introduced lightweight, portable 16 mm cameras. From the concurrence

of political resistance and technological advancement, a fertile epoch of Latin American filmmaking emerged in the early 1960s. In the half-century that followed, it bloomed and ripened into an enduring hemispheric cultural movement.

It has been my privilege to trace the experiences of those filmmakers who lived through the darkest years in their countries, as they recount—and in some ways, testify—in their Academy Visual History Interviews. While several of the artists belong to a younger generation less burdened by oppressive experiences, they too are influenced by a shared geopolitical history. Even the youngest filmmakers we interviewed made references to a time, especially in the mid-1980s, that left an indelible mark on Latin American society and its institutions.

The conditions that gave birth to modern Latin American cinema 50 years ago are evident in overarching themes that continue to unify filmmakers and that are manifest in their narrative work. In their Academy Visual History Interviews, the filmmakers repeatedly cited *storytelling* and its central role in Latin American culture as a force in their work. Interviews revealed how the transmission of stories, whether experienced directly or handed down through generations, has drawn filmmakers to a timeless tradition of orality. Several of the directors recalled stories from their childhood, when maids or grandmothers transfixed them with tales that were at once terrifying and comforting in their familiarity.

Literature, the written descendant of the oral tradition, both chronicles life and liberates its imagination. Invariably the filmmakers emphasized how central literature is to their work, and how the colonial languages of Spanish and Portuguese connect them with literature, with intellectual currents throughout the Americas, and with each other. It is no wonder that so many of the novelists and poets they cited are themselves Latin American, nor that most of these writers are largely unknown to North Americans. I invite you to seek out the writers referenced by the filmmakers, perhaps to discover that their literary storytelling is a precursor to the filmmakers' visual storytelling.

Through our conversations, additional shared themes emerged to distinguish their work as an identifiable body. One such theme is travel. Many of them journeyed to Europe to learn their craft. Others traveled extensively within their own countries and throughout South and Central America, exposing themselves to diverse social and economic strata. Insights gained from traveling deepened and sharpened their cinematic vision.

Another consistent theme is politics, which for Latin American filmmakers, perhaps more than their U.S. counterparts, is an omnipresent force. Several of the filmmakers were forced to flee their home countries while others chose to remain, trying to avoid arrest while making films that subverted the messages of corrupt and repressive governments. Mexican filmmakers were uniquely positioned to benefit from a dynamic pattern of political emigration: Mexico City drew refugees from Franco's war-torn Spain, among them intellectuals, artists, writers, and filmmakers fleeing fascism at home. The interaction among Mexican and Spanish artists stimulated a fiercely engaged cultural life that continues to this day.

In their interviews, they often commented on the business of filmmaking and how institutions and policies have both helped and hindered their careers. In 1979, the first Festival Internacional del Nuevo Cine Latinoamericano, Havana, Cuba drew filmmakers to Cuba, over the years fostering a deep sense of Latin American cinema as a shared entity. Since 1976, the Toronto International Film Festival has been introducing Latin American filmmakers to Europe, the U.S., and Canada. Since its origins in 1978, the Sundance Film Festival has reached out to Latin American filmmakers, with the Sundance Institute helping filmmakers hone their skills through "laboratory" workshops held in the U.S. and Latin America. Such flagship institutions have expanded individual visions while strengthening cross-border alliances.

In contrast, the North American Free Trade Agreement, the 1994 trade pact signed by Mexico, the U.S., and Canada, dealt a blow to the livelihood of Mexican filmmakers as detailed in the Academy Visual History Interviews relayed by Mexican directors Arturo Ripstein and María Novaro. By eliminating quotas that once ensured a place in Mexican movie theaters for Mexican films alongside Hollywood blockbusters, NAFTA had catastrophic economic effects from which Mexican filmmakers are still struggling to recover. Argentina—along with Mexico and Brazil—has one of the strongest film industries in the Americas outside the U.S., yet has also struggled to survive in the face of Hollywood's hegemony, according to the penetrating critique offered by Argentine director and screenwriter Lucrecia Martel.

While many Latin American directors have deliberately kept their distance from Hollywood, over the last decade a few of them have achieved some commercial and critical success here. But given the concentration of Latinos living in California and particularly in Los Angeles, the number of Latin American filmmakers who have "made it" is negligible.

A WORD ABOUT THE ORAL HISTORY PROCESS

The preparations for the oral history interviews mirrored the pre-production phase of my own films. The Academy team and I researched the filmmakers and their works and formulated interview questions which I adapted to my own speaking patterns. A large support cadre included schedulers, intermediaries with the artists and translators, and film crews to record each session. Finally, it was up to me and the interviewees (in two instances with the help of an on-site interviewer) to create the drama within each Academy Visual History Interview. As in documentary filmmaking, the psychological intertwining that takes place during the intimate time shared by the interviewer and subject was paramount.

In my opening statement, I told the interviewees words to the following effect: "I'm not the press. I'm going to ask you some questions, but I'm not here to contradict or judge you. Whatever you say is what you say. It's for your children and grandchildren, for posterity, and for the academics. Make an effort to remember and be as candid as possible. Some of these questions have been asked of you before. Try to think of a fresh response." Then we'd begin. As we delved into their childhoods, their memories were sometimes painful, often tender, and always evocative. They recalled early struggles as they remembered the outset of their careers before proceeding to discuss more recent work.

Previous Page: The Academia Brasileira de Letras in Rio de Janeiro, Brazil, was used as the filming location for the Academy's Visual History with Nelson Pereira dos Santos.

Left: Lourdes Portillo interviews with Sienna McLean-LoGreco in Hollywood, for her own Academy Visual History on December 5, 2013.

I listened and observed intently, trying to read their minds, and interpret their movements.

Although I have experienced it often as a documentary filmmaker, I was exhilarated by the five or six hours of intimacy with these insightful filmmakers. As I was listening and later reading the transcriptions, I sensed the historical value contained within their stories. I hope that these Academy Visual History Interviews, along with others added over time, will be studied, and appreciated by generations of the invisible listeners I imagined gathered behind me as I posed my questions. Toward that end, I have selected a number of statements by the filmmakers made during our conversations, and included excerpts, condensed to reveal insight and character, in the body of this essay.

MEET THE FILMMAKERS

The choice of artists to include in this project derived from a combination of desire, availability, timing, and luck. The selection, with input from the project's Advisory Committee and the Academy team, is not meant to be exhaustive, but is instead a waypoint for the Academy as it broadens the range of filmmakers represented in its ongoing Oral History Project.

Over the course of nearly three years, I (or a designated interviewer) met with and interviewed the following filmmakers to record their oral histories:

THE ELDER

Nelson Pereira dos Santos (1928, São Paulo, Brazil) is an undisputed father of Latin American cinema and a guiding force behind Brazil's Cinema Novo movement. His iconoclastic approach would

have been inconceivable in his boyhood, when most Brazilian films were elaborately staged musicals shot exclusively in studios.

His breakthrough film, *Rio, 40 graus* (*Rio, 100 Degrees F.*, 1955), is a black and white, neorealist portrait of Rio de Janeiro's shantytowns, featuring non-actors. An unblinking look at inequality, racism, and poverty, the film was initially censored by the government, which relented only after widespread public protests. *Como era gostoso o meu Francês* (*How Tasty Was My Little Frenchman*, 1972) is based on several sixteenth-century accounts, including *Brazil: The True History of the Wild, Naked, Fierce, Man-Eating People*, a chronicle by Hans Staden. A captivity narrative that simultaneously critiques and satirizes the Portuguese conquest of Brazil, the film raises pointed questions about the definition of "savage," leading up to its "consuming" finale. He audaciously cast white, middle-class Brazilians, wearing nothing but body paint, beads, and feathers, to play the native Tupinambás, speaking their lines in the Tupi language.

While in Paris as a young man, dos Santos discovered the Cinémathèque française, where he watched at least two films a day. Inspired by neorealism and such filmmakers as Jean Renoir and Jean Vigo, once back in Brazil, he took to the streets wielding a portable 16 mm camera. He filmed shantytowns (*favelas*) and the poor, including black Brazilians, subjects that were then cinematically off limits. Stretching the art form, he inspired young Brazilian filmmakers, including Glauber Rocha and other Cinema Novo co-founders, and other filmmakers internationally.

Still voracious today in his desire to create a Brazilian national cinema that is inclusively Latin American, he envisions a cinema encompassing a range of styles and genres to reveal the continent's contradictions and realities. But in his Academy Visual History Interview, he acknowledged the pervasive influence of Hollywood:

> *American cinema was the great influence, and it has done that to the entire world's cinema, in terms of visual language. Not in content, the content has another influence which is about ideologies and political thought, the world's political moment. It resonates in scenography, in the film, and the way things are filmed.*[1]

FAR FROM HOLLYWOOD

Héctor Babenco (1946, Buenos Aires, Argentina – 2016, São Paulo, Brazil) lived under two dictatorships: in his country of birth, Argentina, and then in Brazil where his family fled. As a Jew, he knew how it felt to be an outsider:

> *I grew up in a setting marked by fear. I was supposed to be called Isaac—Isaque—but . . . I was called Héctor due to a radio play . . . my mother was in love with. And for fear that the name Isaque would unleash attacks on the street because we lived in a neighborhood littered with ex-Nazis. And then we fled to Brazil, leaving everything behind; bedclothes, towels, and just taking with us the clothes on our backs. I remember traveling on the back of that truck in the freezing cold. It seems like a story you'd read by a writer like Gorky. Fleeing . . . is my first memory.*[2]

Like many other filmmakers of his generation, Babenco traveled to Europe, where he learned how to make films by working as an extra in Italian Westerns. Back in Brazil he started seeking out and filming the dispossessed. A young boy living on the streets gave him the idea for *Pixote* (1981), which became an international sensation, even though the film's subject made it a Hollywood outlier. *Kiss of the Spider Woman* (1985), based on the novel by Argentine writer Manuel Puig and starring Raúl Juliá, earned Babenco an Oscar nomination for Best Director.

I am grateful he was able to tell us his story before he died in July 2016.

Left: Director Nelson Pereira dos Santos interviews with Mateus Araujo at the Academia Brasileira de Letras in Rio de Janeiro, Brazil, March 22, 2016.

Right: Director, writer, actor, and producer Héctor Babenco interviews with Mateus Araujo at his home in São Paulo, Brazil, March 25, 2016.

AN EYE FOR TALENT

Bertha Navarro (1943, Mexico City, Mexico) has lived through—and contributed to—the entire span of years covered in the Academy Visual History Interviews. While there are fractionally more women directors in Latin America than in the U.S., Navarro finds herself in an even rarer camp: a woman producer. Her parents, while not wealthy, wanted their children to have culturally rich lives. Her mother insisted that she learn to speak English, and as a child, Navarro traveled with

her father throughout Mexico and, as teenager, with her younger sister throughout Europe.

Navarro began her career as an activist documentary filmmaker, shooting now historic 16 mm footage of the 1968 Tlatelolco Massacre in Mexico City and revolutionary struggles in Chiapas and nearby Nicaragua. She started producing films for her first husband, Mexican filmmaker Paul Leduc (*Reed, México insurgente*, *Reed: Insurgent Mexico*, 1973) and over time stepped into a producing role for other filmmakers.

From early in her career, Navarro promoted and encouraged a new Latin American cinema and its filmmakers. *Cabeza de Vaca* (1991), an early Mexican-Spanish co-production by director Nicolás Echevarría for which Navarro was executive producer, had a talented young make-up artist named Guillermo del Toro on set. Years later, when del Toro asked Navarro to produce his first major feature, *Cronos* (1993), she agreed, and then went on to produce his next two films, *El espinazo del diablo* (*The Devil's Backbone*, 2001) and *El laberinto del fauno* (*Pan's Labyrinth*, 2006). For *Pan's Labyrinth*, she persuaded del Toro to take the same chance she had taken on him with a young Mexican production designer, Eugenio Caballero. Caballero's work earned the film an Academy Award® for Best Art Direction.

Navarro is an advocate for the distinct identity of Latin American cinema:

> There is a kind of cinema . . . that sometimes does have to be very particularly made in Latin America. Social situations . . . where the cultural aspect is important . . . [cinema] is like a historic legacy too, of cultures, because diversity in the world is very important, even though we are all humans and . . . share the same things. But there are ways of understanding them and ways of living them. So . . . for example watching an Iranian film opens up the world to me. At that moment, I can peek into that place, and I believe it is the great, great legacy of cinema.[3]

THE REBELLIOUS SON AND HIS WIFE

Arturo Ripstein (1943, Mexico City, Mexico) grew up in a time when Mexican cinema was staid and repetitive, in part because of his father, a successful film producer. Nepotism took a twist in Ripstein's case. As a teenager, he met Luis Buñuel, then living in Mexico, at a shooting range where the famous director practiced target shooting with Ripstein's father:

> I was . . . 15, I had just watched [Buñuel's film] Nazarin. Dazzled, I went to see him . . . He closed the door and left me outside . . . [I was] really stunned, I had taken

a bus, his house was very far away from where I lived. A moment later he opened the door and said, "Come on in." And in his living room, the curtains were down . . . He had a small projector on the dining table . . . he put on a little roll, he started it and it was Un chien Andalou (An Andalusian Dog, 1929) . . . it's huge, it's amazing, right? The movie ended, and he said to me, 'This is what I do . . .' and I said, 'I want to do the exact same thing.'[4]

His body of work reflects a powerfully realized, mordant view of life. In an early film, *El castillo de la pureza* (*The Castle of Purity*, 1973), a father locks up his wife and children in a house where they are forced to make rat poison for a living. When Ripstein told me that he uses melodrama to revel in the darkness

Left: Producer and director Bertha Navarro interviews with Lourdes Portillo at her home in Mexico City, September 26, 2015.

Right: Director, writer, actor, and producer Arturo Ripstein interviews with Lourdes Portillo at the Centro de Creación Literaria in Mexico City, September 23, 2015.

of the Mexican soul, I understood what he meant: even today we Mexicans, inheritors of twin legacies of the Aztec Empire and Colonial Spain, embrace the darkness of our own reality.

If the language in Ripstein's early features was somewhat rarefied, when **Paz Alicia Garcíadiego** (1949, Mexico City, Mexico) began writing his scripts, she brought the language down to earth, injecting a fatalistic, ironic sense of humor. Her scripts combine indigenous and Spanish culture to capture Mexican colloquialisms. A gifted storyteller like Ripstein (whom she eventually married), Garcíadiego seduces audiences with her tales. She told me:

This [Hungarian gypsy] girl worked at my house . . . and she'd say she would take me to the park, but she'd take me to a movie theater, like three blocks away from my house, where they'd play American movies . . . she was the cacaro's lover; the cacaro was the projectionist. So, all the way down there . . . she would pinch me and throw some white powder in a medallion she had, and she would say some gypsy curse, 'If you tell your grandma where I'm taking you, in flames she'll burn . . . we're gonna stab your mom and your dad is gonna get hit [with a bat]' . . . It was lunch time . . . the theater was empty, and she would go up with the projectionist and do their thing . . . I must have been two and a half years old, I was very little . . . and all alone in that big empty theater . . . half the time I would be scared to death . . . I remember them, Quo Vadis, with Deborah Kerr . . . tied up to a pole, the lion would come up and was about to eat her . . . King Solomon's Mines, when the snake would sneak in

Ava Gardner's boot . . . And there were others that I loved, the musicals . . . With the passing of time, what I know I owe her . . . is that thanks to being all alone, I saw the same movie three, four or ten times, like Shane from Alan Ladd, I think I must have seen it ten times, I loved it, I loved it.[5]

Meanwhile, Latino filmmakers living in California told me stories that were distinctively theirs.

IN LOS ANGELES

Luís Valdez (1940, Delano, California), the son of Mexican-born migrant farmworkers, spent his early childhood on a farm originally owned by a Japanese American farmer who had been relocated to an internment camp after the bombing of Pearl Harbor. Valdez's father ran the farm during the war years, selling its produce to the U.S. Army. Though the farmer never returned after the war, the Valdez family was unable to hold on to the farm when the Army contract ended and resumed their migrant work, traveling throughout California's Central Valley and neighboring states. A brilliant and politically engaged writer and theater director, Valdez founded El Teatro Campesino, long linked to César Chávez and the organizing of the United Farm Workers. Following the success of his play *Zoot Suit*, Valdez refused to sign away script and directing rights. Instead, he sought out a producer for what was to be his dream project—a defiantly Chicano feature film of *Zoot Suit* (1981). He described the film's origins:

> *I had a conception of The Pachuco . . . [as] a superhero. He's mythological, he's Tezcatlipoca actually, Aztec God of the school of hard knocks. That's why he's black and red. But there have never been Chicano superheroes . . . He can fly through the air; he can snap his fingers. So, I was doing that on the set, on the stage; in the movies, I really wanted to actualize it, I wanted him to be on top of a skyscraper, . . . I wanted him to be really cinematically super. And so I wrote that screenplay. And . . . people were saying, 'This is a $20 million movie you're talking about here.' . . . 'No, never get done. Too much. Who do you think you are?' . . . Finally, I get a call from Ned Tanen, president of Universal. He says, 'Come on over and let's talk.' And so we talked, and he says, . . . 'Just film the play.'*[6]

Left: Writer Paz Garcíadiego interviews with Lourdes Portillo at the Centro de Creación Literaria in Mexico City, September 23, 2015.

Right: Director, actor, and writer Luís Valdez with interviewer Lourdes Portillo at the Teatro Campesino in San Juan Bautista, California, June 8, 2014.

Edward Olmos met Luís Valdez during his audition for the part of El Pachuco. Together, the two friends took on Hollywood, Valdez going on to make *La Bamba* (1987) and Olmos getting his next breakthrough when he was cast in the lead role of Robert M. Young's, *The Ballad of Gregorio Cortez* (1982). Olmos rose to a stature rare in Hollywood and almost unprecedented in the experience of Latino audiences in the U.S.: he became one of our most esteemed actors and an activist who claims for us a platform.

Gregory Nava (1949, San Diego, California), a self-described child of the border, belongs to a

Edward James Ólmos (1947, Los Angeles, California), a Chicano like Valdez, played a character named El Pachuco in *Zoot Suit*. Raised in the modest Boyle Heights neighborhood, he and his siblings were taught to dance by their father, who also instilled in them a love of movies:

> [My father would] take us to Hollywood. And we'd go to the Paramount, or we'd go to the Chinese, or we'd go to . . . the Egyptian . . . beautiful theaters. And we would watch, you know, Ten Commandments, we'd watch great movies . . . . And before that, we would just go to the Unique Theatre, on 1st Street. And we'd watch films in Spanish . . . No single artist has influenced me more in my lifetime than Paul Muni did when I saw him perform as Benito Juárez. As Pasteur, as Scarface, as in The Good Earth, a Chinese . . . landlord. He was amazing. If people don't know who he is today, that's sad. But truly a gift of gifts. Probably one of the finest character actors the world has ever seen.[7]

generation of Latinos who went to film school. While he has made several feature films in Hollywood, he is best known today for *El Norte* (1983). Across two years of fundraising for the film, Nava purposefully did not seek financing from film studios for fear of having to relinquish creative control. Eventually *El Norte* received funding from the now discontinued public television anthology series *American Playhouse*. The first American independent film to get an Oscar nomination for Best Screenplay, this Latino-themed film was a theatrical success, in those days an anomaly—all the more so because it featured indigenous protagonists speaking Mayan. Nava admitted that his struggle has been titanic:

> Being a Latino in the film business and knowing what the challenges are, you know . . . they're huge, because there is a glass ceiling, there's prejudice, it's very hard. All of these projects I've made, they took years to make, to rip down the doors, to break through the glass ceilings, to make a film like My Familia . . . Selena . . . Now I see how entrenched the racism is, how tough the attitudes are that you have to break through, I don't have any delusions about being able to change all that anymore.[8]

Hollywood has long been inaccessible to even the most talented and ambitious filmmakers of color—especially those insisting on authenticity in their work. Any film depicting Latinos in their own culture and speaking in their own language stands little chance of being produced commercially. *El Norte* still stands out today as a rarity. The irony is inescapable: the population of Los Angeles is now at least half Latino, but large-budget Hollywood films neither reflect nor serve that population.

WOMEN OF VISION

María Novaro (1951, Mexico City, Mexico) has made a career of defying class and cultural boundaries to make films about economically struggling women and their adventurous incursions into a different kind of life. She told me about her own experiments in resisting the social stratum into which she was born:

> I had a life of strong political militancy . . . I became Maoist . . . right now I think it's very funny, but . . . I was a bourgeois girl that came from a wealthy family, and . . . I did live a process of, like, re-education, of living in conditions in a needy neighborhood,

Far Left: Actor and director Edward James Olmos interviews with Lourdes Portillo at his home in Encino, California, May 15, 2014. Center: Director and writer Gregory Nava discusses his home movies with interviewer Lourdes Portillo at the Academy's Samuel Goldwyn Theater in Beverly Hills, California, June 16, 2015. Right: Director María Novaro interviews with Lourdes Portillo at her home in Mexico City, September 25, 2015.

in very precarious conditions, carrying my water in buckets, living without electricity for a while, things like that, very romantic, in part. But I did get to know Mexico. I did get to know . . . who were the people that live in my country, . . . people I fell in love with and are a part of me.[9]

Novaro joined the Cocina de Imágenes collective, made up of women filmmakers from throughout Latin America. In the wake of second-wave feminism in the U.S., they began making feminist films. Novaro's direction as a filmmaker and screenwriter testifies to her continued commitment to disadvantaged women protagonists while consciously appealing to general audiences. *Danzón* (1991), her most famous film, was able to attract both male and female viewers internationally without sacrificing its feminist perspective.

Novaro was an early attendee of the Sundance Lab for Latin American filmmakers. Though not tempted to make films in Hollywood, she benefited from the feedback she got from Hollywood icons:

I got advice from Sydney Pollack, . . . Paul Mazursky, Redford . . . I also took a directing class with Sigourney Weaver, the actress . . . . at CUEC [Centro Universitario de Estudios Cinematográficos] . . . I never had one actor directing class . . . they didn't exist. Once I was working with [Felipe] Cazals as an assistant. When he called the actors, he would say, 'Bring me the footed props.' . . . It was horrific, and I would say, they are the actors, they aren't footed props! [LAUGHS] But I mean, I really didn't know how to approach actors, and [at Sundance Labs] it was the complete opposite, right? They gave me practical, useful, coherent tools.[10]

Lucrecia Martel (1966, Salta, Argentina) is startlingly creative in turning cinematic conventions upside down. *La mujer sin cabeza* (*The Headless Woman*, 2008), for example, opens on a woman driving down a desolate road in the north of Argentina. Momentarily distracted, she hears a loud thump as she hits something. A more traditional director might show her turning around and then reveal, through her own eyes, what she had hit. But Martel's camera lingers on the woman, who barely reacts. She glances back and reaches for her dark glasses. In a cinematic tour de force, Martel shows the character thinking—and not thinking—as she drives on, unfazed.

In all her work, Martel hints at something deeper, as she suggested in her interview:

There is a tradition in the north [of Argentina] of sleeping a little after lunch . . . And at nap time, so my father could sleep, my grandmother would tell us stories and would try to make us stay still in the room . . . the stories were terrifying. Because they were stories to freeze people with fear . . . Afterwards I found [that] they were stories by Argentinean authors I later read. But what she did . . . was that all the stories were as if they had happened to her or to someone she knew . . . To us, being with my grandmother at nap time and for her to tell us a terrifying story, the situation of being there with her wasn't terrifying, it was very pleasant.[11]

In the course of our conversation, Martel shared her analysis of the relationship between Latin American film and a dominant and domineering Hollywood:

The model for narrative in commercial North American film has permeated the world in a crazy way . . . As a human race, I think we don't have another form of narrating that has been imposed in such a homogeneous way in all the globe. I think that Hollywood cinema must be the first experience that, as a human race, we have of something that has been imposed with such force, right? And it's not always the potency of the story, . . . but the mainstream North American industry is handled as if it were war. The force of penetration, the force with which they impede the growth of regional cinematographic industries is very particular . . . So that Hollywood has always been like a place of childhood melancholy for all of us, because we have been raised watching films about cities and conflicts that are far from us but that in our memory have become ours . . . That's incredible. I think you can only compare this with the force of Greek mythology over culture . . . I'm not comparing the quality but I am indeed comparing the potency . . . On the one hand, there is the war-like force of Hollywood with respect to the industry, but on the other hand the films work on our own memory, and the experiences of other worlds that you have had . . . So, it's odd, it's like a poison candy: a delicious thing that is also deadly.[12]

Left: Director, writer, and producer Lucrecia Martel interviews with Lourdes Portillo at the Academy's Linwood Dunn Theater in Hollywood, California, October 3, 2014.

Alfonso Cuarón (1961, Mexico City, Mexico) makes films in different genres, each one capturing the best of that genre. His eclectic career took off with *Y tu mamá también* (2001), a bittersweet, satirical road movie, followed by an installment in the Harry Potter series, *Harry Potter and the Prisoner of Azkaban* (2004). He went on to direct and write the dystopian *Children of Men* (2006), and his Oscar-winning film *Gravity* (2013) became an overnight classic of the science fiction genre.

Cuarón knew as a child that he wanted to be a movie director:

> As far back as I can remember, I played at making movies. I saw a documentary, a 'making-of,' and that making-of really impressed me because before then, I was a bit confused as to what the director did and what the actors were. It was all the same to me . . . I became aware there was a Sergio Leone, . . . that there was a man that made all the decisions . . . from that moment . . . a Super 8 camera . . . is what I wanted most. And finally, I got it when I was 12 years old. It was a gift from my mother. From then on, I was filming all the time, but without film because the film rolls were too expensive for my family to buy.[14]

Cuarón also knew early on that he wanted to make films for an international audience, a feat more easily accomplished if he made his films in English. Now residing in London with his professional home in Hollywood, he continues to make surprising, artful films in English—although returning to Mexico to make *Roma* in the fall of 2016, his first film since *Y tu mamá también* made in his home country.

HOLLYWOOD CALLING

Patricia Cardoso (1961, Bogotá, Colombia) first came to the U.S. as a Fulbright scholar. After a five-year stint as a Sundance Institute intern, she became the director of its Latin American program. She currently teaches film directing at USC and UCLA. Her popular dramatic comedy *Real Women Have Curves* (2002) should have been the bridge to continued success in Hollywood, but that wasn't to be:

> I am an independent director, that is my identity, I tell movies, what matters to me is to tell a good story. [But] there was a three-year period when I was about to direct seven movies . . . all of them were big-budget movies, 30 million-dollar movies, and in all of those I was one of the two finalists. The way it works in Hollywood is that you're first interviewed by producers. If chosen as a finalist, you're interviewed by the studio executive. I interviewed for seven projects with studio presidents, and out of the seven I was not chosen. The others coincidentally were all men, white and Anglo-Saxon. It was very hard and very difficult to realize that it was almost impossible to get that job.[13]

Left: Director Patricia Cardoso interviews with Lourdes Portillo at the Academy's Linwood Dunn Theater in Los Hollywood, California, April 14, 2015.

Right: Director, writer, producer, and editor Alfonso Cuarón interviews with Lourdes Portillo at the BFI Screening Room in London, England, February 11, 2016.

Alfonso Cuarón and **Alejandro G. Iñárritu** (1963, Mexico City, Mexico) arrived in Hollywood around the same time but from different paths. While Cuarón attended film school, Iñárritu got on-the-job training by filming TV spots in which grabbing and holding the viewer's attention was essential. With his days of making commercials long behind him, his exuberance about filmmaking is palpable. He said of making *The Revenant* (2015):

It was everything. Again, a kind of seduction to be able to find in something so primitive some sort of spiritual exploration, within something as physical, as visceral as vengeance, and as a world as wild and primitive as the beginning of this country,

of ambition, brutality, racism, exploitation of animals, exploitation of nature, exploitation of human beings. That is, the birth of this country is brutal. It is a tremendous colonization. And to tell in some way, in a metaphor, this story. These . . . stories of two men who come from different visions . . . a father of a North American tribe who loses his daughter, a white father who loses his half-blood son . . . So, I was interested in this relationship . . . as a metaphor for the beginning of this country. So, all this to me was new . . . [to] be able to touch something spiritual in the physical, and to be able to understand a new genre and a physicality, grammar . . . How to explore it in a different way? How to be able to make the public live it, not so much with the classic grammar of film, but as a more empathetic experience, more in situ. Through a visual experience. Always for me it was a visual experiment as well. I said, . . . there is a visual symphony, rather than narrative and great dialogues, and great ideas, I think there is a where I was going.[15]

Iñárritu's works often emphasize a harsh form of Mexican realism that tends toward violence and disturbing images, evident in his films *Amores perros* (2000), *Babel* (2006) and *Biutiful* (2010).

Having won Best Director Oscars two years in a row, for *Birdman* or (*The Unexpected Virtue of Ignorance*) (2014) and *The Revenant* (2015), Iñárritu is in the rare and enviable position of being able to make his own kind of films.

EPILOGUE

As much as I have relished this project, I cannot leave it in good conscience without adding that I was disheartened by many of the stories shared by fellow Latino filmmakers who live, as I do, in California. What is true for women filmmakers everywhere is also true here for Latino filmmakers, and especially Latina filmmakers: we face intensified challenges because we still are not welcomed as creative equals. Our stories, our voices, are largely missing from the great American enterprise we call filmmaking.

When several filmmakers said they opted early on to make films in English, I shuddered at the weight of their sacrifice: it speaks of both linguistic and cultural surrender. Most of the interviewees who were born in the U.S. or now reside here told me that they struggle against a tide of rejection, the sense that 'we are rejected because of who we are.' But they do not give up.

I am glad beyond measure that this collection of stories of Latino filmmakers, wherever they live, will have a permanent place of honor in Los Angeles at the Academy of Motion Picture Arts and Sciences, and I thank the Getty Foundation for its foresight in funding the Academy's Latin American cinema exhibition and Oral History Project.

And now with arms outstretched to the future, I offer this repository as a gift and a treasure that rightfully belongs to us all.

LOURDES PORTILLO

Director/Producer

Ms. Portillo has been making award-winning films about Latin American, Mexican, and Chicano/a experiences and social justice issues for nearly thirty years. Her films include *After the Earthquake/Después del terremoto* (1979), the Academy Award® and Emmy® Award nominated *Las Madres: The Mothers of the Plaza de Mayo* (1986), *La ofrenda: The Days of the Dead* (1988), *Columbus on Trial* (1992), *The Devil Never Sleeps* (1994), *Corpus: A Home Movie for Selena* (1999), *My McQueen* (2004), and a short film, *Al Más Allá* (2008). Her feature-length film *Señorita Extraviada* (2001) received a Special Jury Prize at the Sundance Film Festival, Best Documentary at the Havana International Film Festival, the Néstor Almendros Award at the Human Rights Watch Film Festival, and an Ariel, the Mexican Academy of Film Award. Her work has screened at the Venice Biennale, the Toronto, London and São Paulo International Film Festivals, at museums such as the Walker Art Center, the Whitney, the Guggenheim and the Metropolitan Museum of Art, and in the New Directors/New Films program presented by the Film Society at Lincoln Center and the Museum of Modern Art.

NOTES

1. Academy Visual History with Nelson Pereira dos Santos, interviewed by Mateus Araujo in Rio de Janeiro, March 22, 2016.

2. Academy Visual History with Héctor Babenco, interviewed by Mateus Araujo in São Paulo, March 25, 2016.

3. Academy Visual History with Bertha Navarro, interviewed by Lourdes Portillo in Mexico City, September 26, 2015.

4. Academy Visual History with Arturo Ripstein, interviewed by Lourdes Portillo in Mexico City, September 23, 2015.

5. Academy Visual History with Paz Alicia Garcíadiego, interviewed by Lourdes Portillo in Mexico City, September 23, 2015.

6. Academy Visual History with Luís Valdez, interviewed by Lourdes Portillo in San Juan Bautista, June 8, 2014.

7. Academy Visual History with Edward James Olmos, interviewed by Lourdes Portillo in Encino, May 15, 2014.

8. Academy Visual History with Gregory Nava, interviewed by Lourdes Portillo in Beverly Hills, June 16, 2015.

9. Academy Visual History with María Novaro, interviewed by Lourdes Portillo in Mexico City, September 25, 2015.

10. Ibid.

11. Academy Visual History with Lucrecia Martel, interviewed by Lourdes Portillo in Hollywood, October 3, 2014.

12. Ibid.

13. Academy Visual History with Patricia Cardoso, interviewed by Lourdes Portillo in Hollywood, April 14, 2015.

14. Academy Visual History with Alfonso Cuarón, interviewed by Lourdes Portillo in London, February 11, 2016.

15. Academy Visual History with Alejandro G. Iñárritu, interviewed by Lourdes Portillo in Hollywood, September 2, 2016. Quoted excerpt translated by Lourdes Portillo.

IN THE BEGINNING:
FROM LATIN
AMERICA
TO HOLLYWOOD

BY: CARI BEAUCHAMP

"From Latin America to Hollywood" is a bit of a misnomer for this essay on the first few decades of Spanish-language filmmaking and exhibition in Southern California, for Latin American culture and influence were here long before Hollywood was. In fact, Latino influence in Los Angeles stretches back to the mid-1700s when the region was colonized by Spain and Franciscan friars cut a swath through the native villages to build the mission and plaza that formed the city's nucleus. Mexico controlled the territory from 1825 until California was "proclaimed for America" after the Mexican-American War, but while the gold rush that stimulated statehood in 1850 turned San Francisco into a major cosmopolitan city, Los Angeles remained part boomtown, part frontier town through the beginning of the 20th century.

That's when Midwestern families joined together to buy hundreds of acres and moved en masse to the area to create their own communities and infused them with their own values. The Latino residents, even as they were pushed into new neighborhoods, tried to maintain and promote their own culture through church, community and political groups, Spanish-speaking theater, and libraries, and their own newspapers. Their fight was just beginning.

It was into this already multi-ethnic Los Angeles that the "screen machine" was introduced at the Orpheum Theatre in the late 1890s. A larger than life-sized Annabelle Moore was projected onto a sheet to perform her "Sun Dance" for a few precious moments. At the time, movies were a novelty disdained by most and another decade would pass before filmmakers arrived in earnest.[1]

Movie making was a young business, initially driven primarily by immigrant Jews and women — talented, ambitious, and creative souls unwelcomed in respectable professions. If movies were looked down upon as less than reputable—and they were—individuals on the fringes of the filmmaking community were the ones who first came to Los Angeles. They were seeking refuge from "The Trust," the name commonly given to the Motion Picture Patents Company controlled by Thomas Edison, which mandated license fees for the use of its patented cameras and projectors, including the sprocket holes on film. By 1910, there were already 10,000 nickelodeons throughout the country and they were desperate for product. The rising demand for movies and the corresponding increase in theaters made enforcement a challenge; renegade companies fled to Florida and Cuba, but the sun, the dry air, and the ocean drew many to Southern California. Best of all, it was 3,000 miles from New York and the Trust's vigilantes.

Then two events, occurring almost simultaneously, resulted in a cataclysmic shift in this new business of movies. The Trust was beaten in the courts and World War I wreaked havoc on Europe's film industry. Before the assassination in Sarajevo

that started the war, the quality of French and Italian films far surpassed those made in America, but as it progressed, production facilities were shut down and theaters were taken over by occupying armies. By the time of the Armistice, European filmmaking was crippled and American movies dominated the world market. Suddenly, Los Angeles was the international capital of movie making.

The locals of all ethnicities were none too thrilled to see women walking the streets in heavy makeup, men eating lunch under trees in biblical costumes and cameramen using car races, parades, and beach boardwalks as background for their movies. It was a love-hate relationship from the start: as early as 1911, The *Los Angeles Times* editorialized that "the motion picture people may be something of a pest, but their value to the community as national and international advertisers is inestimable."[2]

That didn't deter a group calling themselves "Conscientious Citizens" seeking 10,000 signatures on petitions to drive out "these hoodlums" who had "forced themselves upon our beautiful city to make what they call movies." Signs in front of boarding houses read "No Actors or Dogs." And just as the Anglo elite looked down on these "movies," so did the upper crust of the Latino community. Spanish-language newspapers urged readers to resist this blatant threat to their culture.[3]

Yet, in 1920, filmmaking, and the jobs it brought to the area including tourism, hotels, and restaurants, was declared the primary source of employment in Los Angeles. That same year, over 100 filmmaking companies were listed in the city directory. And what had been greeted with shock and disdain gradually turned to civic pride—appreciated, and depended upon.[4]

Movies were a "cash on the barrel head" business and required relatively little investment. Silent films allowed the producers to simply change the language of the title cards that explained the action, and that efficient and cost-effective system meant that their international profits soared.

While many small companies and individual producers continued to flourish through the mid-1920s, companies began to merge. Marcus Loew, who owned a theater circuit, financed the purchase of the Goldwyn lot in Culver City and brought in Louis B. Mayer to run it, creating MGM. Adolph Zukor and Jesse L. Lasky had originally joined forces in the early teens in Famous Players-Lasky Corporation, but with some wheeling, dealing and kneecapping, they absorbed other investors and companies to turn their distribution arm, Paramount, into a major studio.

From the beginning of filmmaking, the stereotyping of Mexicans as lazy and untrustworthy laced story lines. Among the entrepreneurs who put out shingles as film producers in the 1920s were Guillermo Calles, Manuel R. Ojeda and Manuel Sánchez Valtierra who met with mixed success in combating what they considered North American attempts to "denigrate us unjustifiably." Almost as offensive to some were the films that whitewashed the past, such as D.W. Griffith's one-reeler *Ramona,* made in 1910 and starring Mary Pickford, which used the romance of the mission as a ready background. Los Angeles' Latino heritage was often portrayed as "quaint," blurring the truth by "appropriating and then commercializing their history."[5]

It was an uphill battle, particularly for the Californians, the native-born Spanish and Castilian descendants of those who had once ruled the area. Their numbers and influence waned as the population boomed: in 1910, Los Angeles boasted a population of 300,000 and by 1930, more than one million people called it home.[6]

While they feared assimilation, and resisted the stereotyping of Latinos in films, they were hardly alone in having righteous complaints. African Americans, Jews, even Germans, Italians, and the Irish were often depicted on the screen in derogatory portrayals. Yet for the underemployed minorities of Los Angeles, jobs as extras were alluring, no matter

Previous Page: Portrait of the cast and crew from *La voluntad del muerto* (George Melford and Enrique Tovar Ávalos, 1930), the Spanish-language version of *The Cat Creeps.*

Left: The Founders of the Motion Picture Patents Company, December 18, 1906. Right: Dolores del Río and Warner Baxter in *Ramona* (Edwin Carewe, 1928).

the role to be played. Prior to the creation of the Central Casting office in the mid-1920s, filmmakers in need of "Mexicans and other Hispanic types" counted on two men who created a business out of providing them. Pedro Carmona and Chris-Pin Martin had the extras gather on the corner of Temple and Diamond Streets every morning and wait for jobs that might come. Central Casting established ethnic divisions, but they continued to depend on people such as Carmona and Martin because, as one executive claimed, "Most of these people do not have telephones." Extra work usually meant between $5 and $7.50 a day, but the highlight—according to several who were interviewed later in life—was the lunches. The director Luís Valdez remembers his father telling him about working as a mule driver in the movie *Cimarron* (Wesley Ruggles, 1931). Even though the film went on to win the Best Picture Academy Award in 1931, what Valdez's father praised the most was "how well they ate."[7]

A review of the MGM payroll logs for the 1920s reveals few Latino names in most categories of employment, except for gardeners and the janitorial staff. There were also several Latino names on the list of musicians hired to play on the sets of silent films to set the mood for the actors, but those jobs were just some of the many that would be wiped out by the coming of sound.

THE LATINO STAR EMERGES

Among the major Hollywood stars of the silent era were several Latino actors. The Mexican beauty Dolores del Río was discovered by the director Edwin Carewe as she was dancing in Mexico in 1925. Born Lolita Dolores Martínez Asunsolo López Negrette, she was a stunning twenty-year-old when she met Carewe and ready to leave the marriage she had entered at the age of 15. Carewe immediately put her in his film *Joanna* (1925), and when the studio press praised her as a "Spanish actress," Dolores insisted it be corrected to "Mexican." She then was featured in Raoul Walsh's *What Price Glory?* (1926) and starred as a Russian in *Resurrection* (Edwin Carewe) in 1927; the following year she had her breakout role starring in a feature-length version of *Ramona* (Edwin Carewe, 1928). Her accent remained and hampered her choice of roles in sound films, often limiting her to what was euphemistically referred to as "ethnic and exotic" parts.[8]

She entered the world of the studio social elite by marrying MGM's legendary art director Cedric Gibbons in 1930, and thereafter refused to make Spanish-language films because she feared that they were quickly heading to the category of "B-pictures." She continued to work occasionally and is credited with introducing the two-piece bathing suit to the screen in *Flying Down to Rio* (Thornton Freeland) with Fred Astaire and Ginger Rogers in 1933. But by the early 1940s, she had tired of Hollywood; she divorced Gibbons and returned to Mexico where a flourishing filmmaking community welcomed her.

She starred in *María Candelaria* (1944), directed by the prolific Mexican director Emilio Fernández, whose body of work would come to exemplify the "Golden Era of Mexican Cinema" of the 1940s and '50s. The film won the "Grand Prix" at Cannes in 1946, and the following year John Ford approached her to star in *The Fugitive*, shot in Mexico, co-starring Henry Fonda, and photographed by the renowned Mexican cinematographer Gabriel Figueroa.

Gilbert Roland's story would have been a natural for a Hollywood script. Born Luis Antonio Dámaso de Alonso in Juárez, Mexico, Roland's father, grandfather and great-grandfather had all been matadors, but when Pancho Villa wreaked havoc on their home town, Roland's parents and five siblings all moved to Texas. At 14, Roland left home for Los Angeles, arriving in 1920 and, with his good looks, quickly found work as an extra. His new name was inspired by two famous screen stars, Jack Gilbert and Ruth Roland, and his first featured role was in Clara Bow's 1925 *The Plastic Age* (Wesley Ruggles).The following year he co-starred with Norma Talmadge in *Camille* (Fred Niblo), marking his breakout as a star as well as the breakup of her marriage to producer Joseph Schenck. While the affair played out in the press, Roland was put in Spanish-language films, occasionally playing the stereotypical Mexican bandit. While wanting to work, he resisted being typecast and emerged in the late thirties as a serious character actor in films such as *The Sea Hawk* (Michael Curtiz, 1940), *We Were Strangers* (John Huston, 1949) and *The Bad and the Beautiful* (Vincente Minnelli, 1953). His career eventually took him to television, appearing in two long playing westerns, *The Cisco Kid* and *The High Chaparral*.

Far Left: Extras on the set of *Cimarron* (Wesley Ruggles, 1931). Center Left: Dolores del Río and Cedric Gibbons, undated. Center Right: Dolores del Río and Pedro Armendáriz in *María Candelaria* (Emilio Fernández, 1944). Far Right: Portrait of Gilbert Roland, ca. 1929.

Ramón Novarro was born José Ramón Gil Samaniego in Durango, Mexico, but his family fled the Mexican Revolution and ended up in Los Angeles in 1913. Within four years, the handsome teenager who studied ballet, piano, and singing became an extra in films. It was Rex Ingram who cast him as Rupert in *The Prisoner of Zenda* in 1922 and gave him a new last name. (Payroll records show that as Samaniego he was making $150 a week and as Novarro, his pay jumped to $500 a week.) *Ben-Hur* assured him recognition, stardom, and $1,000 a week by 1925. [9]

According to Novarro's biographer, André Soares, Novarro was MGM's top international male star between 1925 and 1932 while Greta Garbo was the most popular female. Novarro put his singing and dancing skills to use in *Call of the Flesh* (Charles Brabin, 1930), yet while musicals seemed like a natural with sound, their popularity soon faded. Still, Novarro's popularity continued and he defied typecasting. In fact, during his heyday at MGM he never played a character of Mexican descent. Instead he starred as a Frenchman named Armand

(F. Richard Jones, 1927) but her accented English limited her roles in sound films. And when she starred as a Cuban in *The Cuban Love Song* (W. S. Van Dyke, 1931) she was criticized for having a Mexican accent. She tried moving from drama to comedy, but she was more famous for her raging affair with the young Gary Cooper than her roles. She was an outsized personality and in the late 1930s her nickname inspired a series of films with "Mexican Spitfire" in the title. By then she had married and divorced Johnny Weissmuller, making news all the way, but never more so than when she, having become pregnant and rejected by an Austrian actor, committed suicide at the age of 36 in 1944.

THE COMING OF SOUND

When the upcoming film year of 1928 was heralded, no mention was made of sound films. By early summer, *The Jazz Singer,* which had received mixed critical reviews, had been in release for eight months. The film unspooled with traditional title cards used in silent films and calling it melodramatic does not begin to describe this sentimental yarn of generational alienation, mother love and good old show business. *Motion Picture News*

in *Devil-May-Care* (Sidney Franklin, 1929), an Indian named Karim in *Son of India* (Jacques Feyder, 1931), a Russian in *Mata Hari* (George Fitzmaurice, 1931), and an Egyptian in *The Barbarian* (Sam Wood, 1933).

Lupe Vélez, on the other hand, was nothing but stereotyped. "The Mexican Spitfire" found attention starring with Douglas Fairbanks in *The Gaucho*

pronounced it a "nice Jewish picture" of "no great caliber." However, when audiences heard Al Jolson say "you ain't heard nothing yet" straight from the screen before he broke into song, they were not only ecstatic, they kept coming back for more.[10]

Still, many in positions of power continued to dismiss "the current talking picture craze as

nothing more than public curiosity in a novelty." Creatively, the earliest sound films were clunky at best in contrast to the sweeping silent epics such as *The Big Parade* (King Vidor, 1925), *The Winning of Barbara Worth* (Henry King, 1926), and *The Wind* (Victor Seastrom, 1928). The technical advancement in lighting, cinematography and editing had reached the point that film was truly an art form and inserting sound considered a crass distraction. Even "the boy genius," MGM's production head Irving Thalberg, said that "talking pictures are just a passing fad." [11]

Those who had been visionary trailblazers only a decade earlier had not totally lost their touch, rather they were petrified because sound films meant economic and technical changes so vast they didn't even want to contemplate it. The tendency is to look back and assume there was a well-thought-out plan to transition to making film with sound, but all the studios flailed in different ways and went through their own agonizing assessments.

The trades reported that gloom hung over the studios as many closed for as long as two months while a total of seventeen sound studios were constructed throughout the Los Angeles area. By the late summer of 1928, only 400 of the country's 20,000 movie theaters were ready to run sound pictures and theaters in foreign countries were even slower to wire for sound. It was complicated and expensive and once sound did arrive, a new wave of protest and "anti-talkie fury" resulted. If American audiences were disappointed hearing the tenor voice of Jack Gilbert when they had been expecting a deep

Far Left: Poster for *Ben-Hur* (Fred Niblo, 1925).
Middle Left: Costume illustration for *Ben-Hur* (Fred Niblo, 1925).
Center Left: Ramón Novarro, 1921.
Right: Lupe Vélez in *Mexican Spitfire* (Leslie Goodwins, 1940).

baritone, or the Talmadge girls' distinct New York accents, sound was even more disillusioning for foreign viewers. In silent films, their imaginations allowed them to make their own assumptions about the characters on the screen; with sound that was impossible.

As Mary Pickford summarized the situation:

"We of the silent screen enjoyed a unique privilege. Through our voiceless images, we were citizens of every country in the world. And then of course, we made the colossal mistake of opening our mouths and proving how provincial we were. This world citizenship of the screen we threw away with the advent of talk." [12]

SOUND AND THE IMPACT ON FOREIGN MARKETS

While the story lines of silent and talkies were similar, foreign press complained that American films were suddenly a blatant attempt to take over their cultures. Hearing English coming out of the mouths of American actors came across as a new form of colonization. The Mexican novelist Federico Gamboa urged his fellow citizens to "oppose, by all available means, letting [the Yankees] poison us . . . with this pernicious immigration of celluloid men and women." [13]

Foreign language versions had been consistent moneymakers in silent films where translated title cards were easily and cheaply inserted before films were circulated throughout the world. That international business accounted for up to forty percent of studios' eventual revenue and so they were determined to keep up the profits.

At MGM, Irving Thalberg looked around and quickly figured out that no one knew what they were doing so it was most important that he had someone in charge of sound he could trust. He brought his brother-in-law Douglas Shearer from Canada where he had experience in radio to head up MGM's new sound department (Shearer would stay on in that role for decades and his name appears in the credits of hundreds of films).

Sometimes they waited to see what films were hits—in the pivotal year of 1930 MGM went back and remade *The Big House* (George Hill) and *Min and Bill* (George Hill), with Spanish actors after the English-language versions had proven themselves at the box office. But when Greta Garbo was filming her first talkie, *Anna Christie* (Clarence Brown, 1930), she also—simultaneously— made a German version. The rest of the cast and crew were different too since Garbo's popularity in Europe mandated her participation in the darker, foreign version.

Hal Roach tried making the same film in up to five different languages. Internationally popular actors such as Laurel and Hardy made their movies in multiple languages, including Spanish, by taking crash language courses and posting phonetically spelled cue cards around the set.

At Warner Bros, the German Henry Blanke, who would go on to a long career as a producer of such films as *The Adventures of Robin Hood* (Michael Curtiz and William Keighley, 1938), *The Maltese Falcon* (John Huston, 1941), and *Of Human Bondage* (Edmund Goulding, 1946), was put in charge of foreign-language films. One of the first Spanish-language films his department produced was the western, *El hombre malo* (Roberto Guzmán and William C. McGann, 1930) starring Antonio Moreno, a remake

of *The Bad Man* (Clarence G. Badger, 1930), which starred Walter Huston. It was made again as *Lopez, le bandit* (Jean Daumery, 1930) in French; all three versions were released in 1930.

Fox tried adding subtitles, but they were often poorly translated and didn't sync with the English dialogue. Just as Hollywood studios ravaged Broadway for stage-trained actors capable of enunciating clearly, they brought in Spanish-speaking actors from regional theater and beyond for casting in Spanish versions as well as to dub films. Dubbing was used for a while as a substitute for the expensive and time-consuming practice of filming versions of the same film in several different languages, yet the translations often left much to be desired and a mix of accents didn't help.

At Universal, the Czech-born Paul Kohner was assigned the task of making foreign-language films at night, saving money by using the same sets on the same sound stages used to make English-speaking films by day. Kohner also had an ulterior motive because he had his eye on the studio's latest ingénue.

Lupita Tovar had been a high school student in Mexico City when a talent scout from Fox came across her in gym class. She recalled she was wearing "my enormous, black bloomers below my knees, with black stockings and my tennis shoes," but her doe-eyed beauty shone through. Lupita had never seen a camera before, but Fox was obviously impressed with what they saw in her screen test because within weeks she was offered $300 and a contract. She arrived in Los Angeles with "my school clothes and a little satchel," accompanied by her grandmother. [14]

Fox might have had big plans for Tovar, but she spoke little English so after appearing in small parts,

Antonio Moreno in *El hombre malo* (Roberto E. Guzmán and William C. McGann, 1930).

41

she was sent to Universal where she was put to work dubbing. Confused and feeling lonely, Lupita was ready to go home, but then Paul Kohner arranged to have her cast opposite Antonio Moreno in the 1930s film *La voluntad del muerto* (George Melford and Enrique Tovar Ávalos, 1930), the Spanish-language version of *The Cat Creeps* (Rupert Julian and John Willard, 1930).

That was followed the next year by one of the most famous of all Spanish-language films, *Drácula* (George Melford, 1931), which is often praised as superior to the English version. During the day, the director Tod Browning, cinematographer Karl Freund and stars Bela Lugosi and Helen Chandler made their film and in the early evening, a new crew came in and reset the cobwebs in the sets designed by John Hoffman, Herman Rosse and Charles Hall.

The director George Melford (who spoke no Spanish), cinematographer George Robinson, and stars Lupita Tovar and Carlos Villarías went to work after dark using the same props, matte painting and sets. Villarías reportedly even used Lugosi's widow's peak toupee. One difference however was that Tovar's costumes were much more revealing than Chandler's.

The Spanish *Drácula* was almost half an hour longer, allowing for more character development, lingering close-ups as well as more dialogue and dramatic camera movement. Melford also had the presumed advantage of watching Browning's rushes. The English version was budgeted at $350,000 and the Spanish version was listed as costing around $65,000, but of course sets and costumes were all billed to the English version. Just the same, the lower salaries of the cast and crew of the Spanish version are reflected in the lower budget.

Foreign-language sound films also resulted in changes in exhibition and distribution. Where there had once been hundreds of distribution companies, the growth of studios meant the consolidation of distribution under their umbrella. Now that films were more expensive, more thought was given to how they were released. Prints were sent to the closest and most remunerative cities first, then gradually farther and farther and farther afield (one of the reasons that so many "lost" films have been found in places such as Australia is that they were the last stop for print distribution and it often wasn't worth the cost of shipping to return them).

Hoping to seize on the new hunger for sound films in Spanish, Francisco Fource became Southern California's Spanish-language Sid Grauman. Fource, born to Spanish parents in Hawaii, took over the 2,000-seat Teatro California on Main and Eighth Streets in 1932. He then created a "circuit" of sorts, adding the Hidalgo and Electric Theaters under his management. At the time, it was a big risk to enter the fray as the quality of the product was unreliable. Yet, just as Hollywood was giving up on making profitable, multiple-language films, Mexico began its own film production in earnest.

SOUND FILM PRODUCTION IN MEXICO

Santa (Antonio Moreno, 1932) is heralded as the first major sound film made in Mexico, marking the beginning of what would become a burgeoning industry for the country and the end of the Mexican talent migration to Hollywood. However, at the time, the making of the film was anything but auspicious. Starring Lupita Tovar, *Santa* was directed by the established star Antonio Moreno who had never directed before. He was assisted by a Cuban, Ramón Peón. The supporting cast included Mimí Derba and Carlos Orellana in his first film and it would feature music by Agustín Lara.

Tovar returned to her home country after an absence of several years, hoping to be welcomed with open arms. Her other films had screened in Mexico and her popularity was established, but she hadn't factored in the purpose of her trip: to star in *Santa*. She had not read the famed novel by Federico Gamboa so she assumed that as the title character, she would be playing a saint. Her father, however, knew the book and that she was cast as a prostitute, so instead of greeting his daughter as a returning heroine, he kicked her out of the house. Ironically, Lupita, who was still struggling with her English, went with her grandmother to live at an English-language school. (Following the completion of *Santa,* Tovar returned to Hollywood, married Paul Kohner, and they stayed happily together until his death in 1988.)

Left: Carlos Villar (later Villarias) and Lupita Tovar in *Drácula* (George Melford, 1931).

Right: Portrait of Lupita Tovar, ca. 1931.

The interiors of *Santa* were filmed at an abandoned silent film studio at the entrance of Chapultepec, Mexico City's large and very noisy park. The cinematographer, Alex Phillips, wrapped his cameras in blankets and old mattresses to muffle the sound. (Phillips arrived not speaking a word of Spanish, but stayed on in Mexico for the rest of his life making over 100 films there.) The sound engineers were Joselito and Roberto Rodríguez who had come to Hollywood from Mexico and devised what became known as "The Rodríguez Brothers Sound System," recording sound on film in such a compact way they were able to operate out of a van. (They, and their younger brother Ismael, would also stay in Mexico and become successful and prolific writers/producers/directors.)

Tovar and Moreno were fêted at the *Santa* premiere at the Teatro California in Hollywood. The grand event was hosted by José Mojica, a star of Spanish-language films, and celebrities such as Laurel and Hardy were in attendance. Both the opening and the run of the film were big successes, but soon the theater returned to screening Hollywood-made films. Other "Made in Mexico" films began to trickle in to Los Angeles, and the Teatro Mexico pushed cultural celebration to a new high when it reopened on Mexican Independence Day in 1932 with an interior that boasted Mexican flags and the screening of *Contrabando* (Alberto Méndez Bernal and Frank Wells), advertised as "spoken entirely in Spanish, made in Mexico, with Mexican capital, and with Mexican actors and direction as well." The Mexican film industry was beginning to establish itself as an alternative to Hollywood-produced Spanish-language films.[15]

"THE DECLINE OF SPANISH-LANGUAGE PRODUCTION IN HOLLYWOOD"

The conversion to sound had required an influx of money and Wall Street seriously invested, but by the early 1930s, the Depression had circled the world and hit Hollywood with a wallop. There were so many mergers, bankruptcies and consolidations that only seven major studios remained from the more than 100 filmmaking companies that had existed in 1920. Attention to the bottom line was paramount and costs were cut across the board. The already poorly funded foreign language films suffered as a result, and the inconsistent success of Spanish-language films and the theaters where they were screened was not unlike the other movie theaters that populated the area. With so many challenges, providing films in multiple languages simply did not bring enough profit to warrant the attention of the Louis B. Mayers or the Adolph Zukors.

By the mid-1930s, Spanish-speaking films for American audiences were coming from Mexico, Argentina, and Spain. Firms such as Azteca Films and then Clasa-Mohme, Inc. distributed Mexican-made sound films to the U.S. and Spanish-speaking countries. Within a few years, Mexican filmmaking had developed to the point that they provided "U.S. theaters with approximately ninety percent of their booking needs in the Spanish language."[16]

As filmmaking came into its own in countries such as Spain, Mexico, and Argentina, they found themselves with a local industry to promote and protect. By 1940, higher taxes and tariffs were instituted and Hollywood faced limits on the number of their films that could be exported. Ironically, as movie making was consolidated into a reduced number of large studios in Los Angeles, small independent companies were flourishing in other countries, providing films in their native language for themselves and the rest of the world.

With all the changes that Hollywood was going through, one thing didn't change: the stereotypical representation of Latinos in Hollywood films. Such depictions were commonplace in part because of the few Latinos working behind the camera. No one seemed to notice, but of course they did. Eventually, questions began to be raised and alternative voices heard, and it is a battle that continues to this day.

CARI BEAUCHAMP

Author and Film Historian, Los Angeles, CA

Ms. Beauchamp is the award-winning author of *Without Lying Down: Frances Marion and the Powerful Women of Early Hollywood* and five other books of film history. Her books have been selected for "Best of the Year" lists by the *New York Times*, the *Los Angeles Times*, and Amazon. She writes for *Vanity Fair*, appears on Turner Classic Movies and in multiple documentaries and is the only person to twice be named an Academy of Motion Pictures Arts and Sciences Scholar. She has also written and produced documentaries. Cari currently serves as the Resident Scholar for the Mary Pickford Foundation Member and on the Advisory Board of the Center for the Study of Women in Television and Film.

Left: Poster for Santa
(Antonio Moreno, 1952).

NOTES

1. David Nasaw, "Learning to Go to the Movies," *American Heritage* (November 1993), 79–80.

2. *Los Angeles Times*, January 17, 1911.

3. Cari Beauchamp, *Without Lying Down: Frances Marion and the Powerful Women of Early Hollywood* (Berkeley: UC Press, 1998), 27–28.

4. Lewis Jacobs, *The Rise of the American Film* (New York: Harcourt, Brace, 1939), 160–61; 100 companies, Los Angeles Directory, 1920.

5. Colin Gunckel, *Mexico on Main Street: Transitional Film Culture in Los Angeles Before World War II* (New Brunswick, N.J.: Rutgers University Press, 2015), 55; George J. Sánchez, *Becoming Mexican American: Ethnicity, Culture and Identity in Chicano Los Angeles 1900–1945* (New York: Oxford University Press, 1995), 70.

6. *Film Daily*, August 8, 1928.

7. Anthony Slide, *Hollywood Unknowns: A History of Extras, Bit Players and Stand-Ins* (Jacksonville: University of Mississippi, 2012); Academy Visual History with Luís Valdez, interviewed by Lourdes Portillo in San Juan Bautista, June 8, 2014.

8. *New York Times*, April 13, 1983.

9. Novarro pay records, *Metro-Goldwyn-Mayer Accounting Department records, 1917–1969*, Margaret Herrick Library Special Collections, Los Angeles, no. 227.

10. A. Scott Berg, *Goldwyn: A Biography* (New York: Ballantine Books, 1989), 173; "New Year Finds Hollywood Busy," *Film Daily*, January 3, 1928; *Film Daily*, December 2, 1927; After opening in New York, The *Jazz Singer* continued playing for months and cities such as Chicago and Los Angeles had similar results *Film Daily*, February 16, 1928. Al Jolson had been a last-minute replacement for George Jessel who had "balked when he learned he was expected to sing, pointing out his contract called only for his appearance" (*Film Daily* May 26, 1927). Sam Warner, the brother credited with being the biggest advocate for sound, died of a sinus infection at the age of 40 the week The *Jazz Singer* opened (*Variety*, October 6, 1927).

11. *Motion Picture News*, August 11, 1928; Samuel Marx, *Mayer and Thalberg: The Make Believe Saints* (New York: Random House, 1975), 100, 105. When MGM first announced their plans for 1928, all fifty films were to be silent.

12. Mary Pickford, *This Life* (draft of manuscript that would become her autobiography, *Sunshine and Shadow* [New York: Doubleday, 1955]), pt. 2, 285.

13. *Film Daily*, July 22, 1928 and *Film Daily*, August 5, 1928; *Film Daily*, September 9, 1928; Lisa Jarvinen, *The Rise of Spanish-Language Filmmaking: Out from Hollywood's Shadow, 1929–1939* (New Brunswick, N.J.: Rutgers University Press, 2012).

14. Academy interview with Lupita Tovar at "A Salute to Lupita Tovar," interviewed by Ellen Harrington, Los Angeles, December 7, 2006.

15. Colin Gunckel, *Mexico on Main Street: Transitional Film Culture in Los Angeles Before World War II* (New Brunswick, N.J.: Rutgers University Press, 2015), 126.

16. Rogelio Agrasánchez, Jr., *Mexican Movies in the United States: A History of the Films, Theaters, and Audiences, 1920–1960* (Jefferson, N.C.: McFarland & Co., 2006), 161.

THE NEW LATIN AMERICAN CINEMA MOVEMENT: INFLUENCES RECEIVED, SHARED, AND GIVEN

BY: JOSÉ SÁNCHEZ-H.

"DISCOVERING" LATIN AMERICAN CINEMA

The New Latin American Cinema was "discovered" in Europe in the 1960s with the Great Young Filmmakers Award given to Bolivia's Jorge Sanjinés for his film *Ukamau* (a word in the language of the Aymara people of the Andes expressing *That's the Way It Is*, 1966) and the Best Director Award given to Brazil's Glauber Rocha for *O dragão da maldade contra o Santo Guerreiro* (*Antonio das Mortes*, 1969), both at the Cannes Film Festival. This movement was born out of the filmmakers' desire to create a new cinema that would reflect the reality of what was happening in their countries. According to Nancy Caro Hollander, "the New Latin American Cinema movement . . . emerged in the cultural ferment from the late 1960s to produce feature films for Latin American audiences that explored the historical forces responsible for poverty, class antagonisms, and political repression."[1] The work of Sanjinés and Rocha, as well as other filmmakers like Cuba's Tomás Gutiérrez Alea (*Memorias del subdesarrollo/Memories of Underdevelopment*, 1968), provoked thought by not conforming to European or Hollywood cinema.

This essay will explore some of the influences received, shared, and given by the New Latin American Cinema movement, focusing

primarily on the period from the 1960s to the 1980s. The films addressed have been selected to illustrate recurring themes in the work of both Latin American filmmakers and Latino filmmakers in Los Angeles. Two essential themes developed by the New Latin American Cinema movement are reclaiming cultural

identity, and film as an expression of historical reality. Jorge Ruffinelli's statement about the documentary *La batalla de Chile* (*The Battle of Chile*, 1975, 1976, and 1979) by Patricio Guzmán is relevant: "Without this film, perhaps those years would not exist."[2] Finally, the section on influences given will consider how the New Latin American Cinema movement has had an impact on Los Angeles in particular, and the United States in general.

INFLUENCES RECEIVED

FILM INFLUENCES ON THE NEW LATIN AMERICAN CINEMA

In the 1960s, Latin American filmmakers developed a realist cinema that used experimentation to create authentic images. The New Latin American Cinema movement, which includes Brazil's Cinema Novo, was influenced by the cinema of India's Satyajit Ray as well as films from Hollywood and the French New Wave. Another strong influence was Italian neorealism, particularly in its humanistic approach to the development of characters and stories.[3]

Latin American filmmakers adapted neorealism to fit their specific situations. Rejecting the hegemony of Hollywood style, these filmmakers sought a new cinematic language. While it was only in Argentina, Brazil, and Mexico that studios were even available, this

cinematic movement took the camera to authentic locations, some of them remote. Also, in the interest of authenticity, nonprofessional actors were cast in leading roles. Stories focused on the current situation, as well as reclaiming history and identity, and represented social classes that had not seen themselves mirrored before on the film screen. One aspect of constructing Latin American consciousness was deconstructing colonization, including at the level of cinematic language. Reflecting the varying realities of different Latin American countries, the theoretical approaches varied as well: Argentina's "Third Cinema"; Bolivia's "Cinema close to the people"; Brazil's "Aesthetics of Hunger"; Cuba's "Imperfect Cinema."[4]

The influence of Jean-Luc Godard and the French New Wave can be seen in the New Latin American Cinema in the way filmmakers use new and different narrative forms to communicate.[5] Jorge Sanjinés states: "A film about the people made by a screenwriter isn't the same as a film made by the people *through* a screenwriter, inasmuch as the interpreter and translator of that people becomes their expressive vehicle. With a change in the relations of creation comes a change in the content and, in parallel, a change in the form."[6]

In 1958 the First Latin American Meeting of Independent Filmmakers was held in conjunction with the SODRE film festival in Montevideo, Uruguay. The delegates included Argentina's Fernando Birri and Leopoldo Torre Nilsson, Bolivia's Jorge Ruiz, Brazil's Nelson Pereira dos Santos, Chile's Patricio Kaulen, Peru's Manuel Chambi, and Uruguay's Danilo Trelles and Roberto Gardiol. Adopting resolutions addressing challenges they had in common, they sought to create a "cinema that could help Latin America take on 'the inevitable task of protecting its education, culture, history, tradition, and working for the spiritual elevation of the population.'"[7]

Whereas the Latin American documentaries of the fifties mainly followed the ethnographic model, these filmmakers took on creating images of social reality unlike any seen before.[8] The foundations of this shift comprised a range of influences and experiences, including neorealism and the Griersonian documentary.[9] Some examples of this shift are Ruiz's *Vuelve Sebastiana* (*Come Back, Sebastiana*, 1953), Pereira dos Santos's *Rio, 40 graus* (*Rio, 100*

Degrees F., 1955), and Birri's *Tire dié* (*Throw Me a Dime*, 1958/1960).[10] In his Academy Visual History Interview, Pereira dos Santos mentions how he was influenced by neorealism: "My head was evidently full of neorealism, so I had to make this film." He goes on to say: "But the greatest novelty is the presence of poor people, of the Shantytown, and of black people. Because . . . they used to say . . . it wasn't cinematographic."[11]

In 1992 at the Festival des 3 Continents in Nantes, France, *Come back, Sebastiana* was recognized as the first indigenous film made in Latin America, and Ruiz was declared the "father of indigenous Andean cinema." Ruiz described himself as a disciple of Robert Flaherty and John Grierson, particularly in his early work such as *Virgen India* (*Indian Virgin*, 1948). He considered American filmmaker Willard Van Dyke as an influence. Another influence was Mexican director Emilio Fernández and his cinematographer Gabriel Figueroa, especially their first two collaborations on *María Candelaria* (1943) and *Flor silvestre* (*Wildflower*, 1943). Their work together created powerful visual narratives, in which the indigenous world was idealized. Fernández and Figueroa in turn drew inspiration from Sergei Eisenstein's unfinished film *¡Que viva México!* (*Thunder over Mexico*, 1932).[12] Eisenstein combined folk images with stylistic elements of contemporary Mexican artists.[13]

Juan Pablo Avila-Ramírez writes that *Come Back, Sebastiana* is a precursor film to the New Latin American Cinema movement and inspired filmmakers such as Jorge Sanjinés to work on films that dealt with Andean cultures.[14] Although often referred to as an ethnographic documentary, the film blends elements of both documentary and narrative approaches. Events are recreated and played by non-actors who, though not the actual participants of the story, are representing the history of their community. Ruiz traveled to Santa Ana de Chipaya in the *altiplano* (Andean high plain), where the indigenous Chipaya community was on the verge of dying out. He gathered stories that had happened in their community, with the intention of making a film. The story that impressed him the most was about a twelve-year-old Chipaya girl. Although attracted to an Aymara town with more resources, she chooses to reclaim her cultural identity.[15]

Ruiz's film explores complex social realities of Andean cultures while creating visually poetic images. Although Ruiz had begun using sync sound on *Bolivia busca la verdad* (*Bolivia Seeks the Truth*, 1950), on this film he used narration with the feel of a storyteller. Perhaps this is one reason why the film has been seen as a documentary. *Come Back, Sebastiana* has characteristics of neorealism in using indigenous non-actors to reconstruct actual events in actual locations.

Historian Carlos Mesa Gisbert, who served as President of Bolivia from 2003 to 2005, addresses the significance of the film by saying, "Sebastiana returns. She returns to the origins of her culture. Here is a valid ideological awareness for the Bolivian nation itself, precisely at the moment of the emergence of a new collective thinking."[16] Historian/filmmaker Alfonso Gumucio Dagrón states: "*Come Back, Sebastiana* places the foundation for the birth of a new Bolivian cinema, and certainly leads the cinema being made in other parts of the continent in that period."[17]

JORGE SANJINÉS: MAKING FILMS CLOSE TO THE PEOPLE

The influence that *Come Back, Sebastiana* had on other filmmakers includes Jorge Sanjinés. In a Cuban magazine article, Sanjinés mentions that he considers *Come Back, Sebastiana* as an antecedent to his own cinematographic work.[18] Director Sanjinés, scriptwriter Oscar Soria, and producer Ricardo Rada formed the production company Ukamau Ltd.; the "Ukamau experience" refers to the New Bolivian Cinema created by Sanjinés. Much of his work deals with moral indignation and denounces social injustice. *Yawar mallku* (*Blood of the Condor*, 1969), considered by UNESCO as the fifty-ninth most important film in the history of cinema, dealt with the sterilization of indigenous women without their consent.[19]

According to Sanjinés, at the ending of *Blood of the Condor* when Sixto—a character who has assimilated into Spanish society—returns wearing indigenous clothing, it is not merely an exaltation of the indigenous. Sixto does not renounce his worker condition, but assumes his cultural identity as a weapon of resistance. His return is also a symbol of the workers' and peasants' unity. Class struggle has been raised.[20] John Hess states that in the resolution of Sixto's story, "we see a Quechua who had tried to assimilate into Spanish Bolivian society return to his Quechua identity—in a sense we see the decolonization of a mind."[21]

Among his influences, Sanjinés recognizes directors Satyajit Ray, Italy's Francesco Rosi, and Theo Angelopoulos from Greece. Two films that made a deep impression on him are *Salvatore Giuliano* (1962) by Rosi and *Pather Panchali* (1955) by Ray.[22] Sanjinés writes: "Since ours was a cinema which sought to develop parallel to historical evolution, but which also sought to influence the historical process and to extract its constitutive elements, it could no longer confine itself to conventional forms and structures. Such content demanded a complementary form which would break traditional molds . . . If it was absolutely necessary to work with reality and the truth, manipulating live, everyday history, it was for the same reasons absolutely necessary to find forms which would not detract from or betray their content."[23]

Considered one of the most important films of the New Latin American Cinema, Sanjinés' *El coraje del pueblo* (*The Courage of the People*, 1971) deals with historical reconstruction and popular memory. The film reconstructs a massacre that occurred on June 24, 1967 in the mining town of Siglo XX. The Ukamau Group collaborated with some of the survivors of the massacre to document this repressive action of the government against the Bolivian people.[24] This represents Sanjinés's approach of making films alongside the people by allowing the community to have a voice through his filmmaking.[25]

La nación clandestina (*The Clandestine Nation*, 1989) continues developing the theme of reclaiming cultural identity posed by Ruiz in *Come Back, Sebastiana* and explored by Sanjinés in *Blood of the Condor*. Sebastian has been expelled from his Aymara community in the *altiplano* and leads an empty, drunken life in La Paz. He undertakes a journey back to his community, seeking redemption for his corrupt actions by sacrificing his life for the good of the community in a sacred ritual of dancing to death. The sacrificial image is intensified by the heavy ceremonial mask strapped to his back. As he travels from the city through the majestic landscape, Sebastian travels through his memories, which are presented as flashbacks.[26]

Sanjinés's films using indigenous non-actors playing themselves contrast with the films by Emilio Fernández, where indigenous characters were played by movie stars, including María Félix, Dolores del Río, and Pedro Armendáriz. The European-based visual language used in early films, such as *That's the*

Way It Is and *Blood of the Condor*, was less effective in reaching his intended audience who were the workers, miners, and peasants. His new visual approach of filming fluid master shots (long takes with camera movement) which he began using in *The Courage of the People*, was better received. The use of fluid master shots in *The Clandestine Nation* is "the more adequate narrative resource for visual translation of the circular conception of Aymara time, as well as of the indestructible bond of the individual from this culture with his social and natural environment."[27]

Left: Director Nelson Pereira dos Santos on set, undated.

Right: Production still of *La nación clandestina* (*The Clandestine Nation*, Jorge Sanjinés, 1989).

SHARED INFLUENCES

CUBA AS A SITE OF CULTURAL EXCHANGE BETWEEN LATIN AMERICA AND LOS ANGELES

During the 1960s and 1970s, Cuba provided a hub of connection between Latin America and Latinos in the U.S.[28] For example, in 1964 Luís Valdez traveled to Cuba with a group called the Student Committee for Travel to Cuba. In his Academy Visual History Interview, conducted as part of the *Pacific Standard Time: LA/LA* project, he talks about the effect of the trip: "The revolution was only five years old. And it was hopeful, and youthful, and it created Latin America for me, it opened my eyes to the fact that I was really a Latin American, Latino, you know in that sense. Really in a worldwide sense."[29]

At that time, Latin American filmmakers felt the need to have their own film festival that could provide common ground for filmmakers from Latin America and other countries. Director Jesús Treviño served on the Cuban-sponsored Latin American Filmmakers Committee, which helped to develop the festival. The committee's declaration regarding the festival defined the connection between the New Latin American Cinema movement and Chicano filmmakers: "We also declare our solidarity with the struggle of Chicano cinema, the cultural manifestation of a community that combats the oppression and discrimination within the United States in order to affirm its Latin American roots."[30]

The first festival in Havana in December 1979 was attended by a delegation of Chicano filmmakers. Treviño states: "It was a real eye-opener experience for a lot of Chicanos that went, because for the first time they were seeing a lot of Latin American, not just Cuban, cinema."[31] The New Latin American Cinema presented in Cuba unveiled for Chicano filmmakers that the struggle for social justice was also an issue of their counterparts in Latin America, among whom one of the most influential was Sanjinés. Festival president Alfredo Guevara states: "We can never forget that eminent figure of the cinema of consciousness and combat that is Jorge Sanjinés."[32] According to Chon A. Noriega, the alliance with the New Latin American Cinema helped Chicano cinema to develop in opposition to Hollywood while aspiring to enter the mainstream. He writes, "Chicano cinema both juxtaposed and straddled two locations: America and América."[33]

LA/LA COMMON THEMES

Amid the cultural ferment and political awakening of the 1960s through the '80s, filmmakers on both American continents were exploring some common themes in their work. Numerous shared influences, along with personal experience, informed the humanistic films they wanted to make.[34]

As in the films of Ruiz and Sanjinés, the theme of indigenous communities reclaiming their cultural identity emerges in Chicano cinema with Luís Valdez' *I Am Joaquin* (1969). The work of Luís Valdez with the Teatro Campesino, similar to the "Ukamau experience" in Bolivia, developed the role of the artist in society as one of raising consciousness and expressing historical reality. In the 1960s and 1970s, Sanjinés and the Ukamau Group traveled in Bolivia with their 16 mm film projectors to indigenous communities, enabling indigenous people to see their own reality on screen.

Both of these filmmakers also focused on expressing historical reality through films that created historical reconstructions: Sanjinés in *The Courage of the People* and Valdez in *Zoot Suit* (1981). As Sanjinés puts it: "Film and politics are for us—and I am speaking in the name of the group that I work with—one and the same thing. Politics is inherent in fundamental human activity, and the commitment of the artist in confronting the social problems that surround him inevitably defines him, from the political point of view. The deeper his commitment, the greater political significance his work will acquire."[35]

Noriega discusses how Chicano films, which were often viewed by audiences with direct experience of the subject matter, served as a form of community building. This function was more crucial than the formal aspects of the films or finding mass distribution. He also mentions the Chicano Movement's call, iterated in "El Plan Espiritual de Aztlán," for cultural expressions to "strengthen our identity."[36]

LUÍS VALDEZ AND EL TEATRO CAMPESINO

In 1962, the United Farm Workers (UFW) was founded. In 1965 the UFW gained national attention, under the leadership of César Chávez, when it participated in the grape strike in Delano, California. To support the striking farmworkers, Luís Valdez created El Teatro Campesino. The group's collaborative skits, called *actos*, used the flatbeds of trucks as a stage.[37] Valdez describes the actos as political acts. He based them on the *autos sacramentales* used by Spanish priests to convert indigenous people to Christianity. Traditional in Spain, these short pieces were stagings of the liturgy. He adapted this approach into *actos argumentales*, in which the through line was an aspect of the strike.

In a parallel with the New Latin American Cinema, Valdez talks about his experience of working with non-professional actors, including Felipe Cantu, a campesino from Nuevo León, Mexico. Though brought in as a scab, he joined the strike then became part of the Teatro. Felipe had a wealth of ideas and contributed to the improvisations.[38]

In 1967 "I Am Joaquin," the Chicano Movement poem by Rodolfo "Corky" Gonzales, was performed live as a slide show by the Teatro Campesino.[39] In 1969 Luís Valdez directed the film adaptation of this epic poem, which addresses five centuries of Chicano history starting with Spain's conquest of Mexico and including the colonial period, Mexico's Independence from Spain, the Mexican Revolution, and the Chicano Movement. *I Am Joaquin* integrates conflicting aspects of the conquered/conqueror and indigenous/Spanish dichotomies to forge a "collective historical identity for Chicanos."[40] Among Chicano Movement artists, Valdez was in the vanguard of highlighting the indigenous legacy and de-emphasizing the European heritage of Chicano people. In

1968 he explained: "It is not enough to say we suffer an identity crisis, because the crisis has been our way of life for the last five hundred years."[41]

Film scholar Rosa-Linda Fregoso differentiates Chicanos as re-affirming "their connections to their indigenous ancestors," rather than their Spanish lineage as prior generations of Mexican Americans

had.[42] According to John R. Chavez: "Chicanos increasingly saw a parallel between themselves and the native peoples of other colonized lands: all had been conquered, all had been reduced to menial labor,

Director Luís Valdez during his involvement in the Delano Grape Strike as founder of the Teatro Campesino, 1966.

53

throughout the Chicano organizations, and it seemed to have a similar response, you know, wherever it was shown . . . I think for Chicanos, it was a very special awakening."[45]

Valdez speaks about the importance of historical reconstructions in theater and film: "Shakespeare had his histories . . . I think that the . . . link between theater and history is very important. That you need reenactments of historical events, in order to understand the sequence of the events that led to today. What is it that makes us what we are today? . . . *Zoot Suit* for instance, is a *historia*."[46]

Written and directed by Valdez and based on his play, *Zoot Suit* addresses both historical reconstruction and reclamation of cultural identity. The story brings together two incidents from Los Angeles history: the 1942 Sleepy Lagoon murder case and the 1943 "Zoot Suit Riots." In the case of a murdered Chicano, twelve of the seventeen young Chicanos convicted were given life sentences. Eventually the convictions were overturned. In the riots, Chicanos who dressed in stylized zoot suits were targeted and beaten by U.S. sailors.[47] Regarding both incidents, Valdez's film serves as a critique of the "official story."[48]

Zoot Suit retains stylized elements of the play: filmed in the theater, it includes shots of the audience. Musical numbers and flashbacks tell the story, narrated by El Pachuco who is only visible to protagonist Henry Reyna and the audience. Valdez describes El Pachuco as a mythical figure of "an archetypal rebel with Native American roots." He sees the Pachuco as Henry's super-ego: "the Pachuco is also goading Henry into a greater level of self-consciousness . . . he represents what Pachuquismo is all about, which is this struggle for identity."[49] Further, the Pachuco brings in elements of Brechtian theater,

and all had been used to extract the natural bounty of their own land for the benefit of the conqueror."[43]

Similar to the work of Sanjinés, the film was shown to an audience that it directly represented, both at rallies of farmworkers and in urban neighborhoods. It also spread to a wider audience through classrooms, festivals, and national television.[44] Valdez remembers: "How great that it can have this kind of impact. It circulated very quickly,

as well as Godard and other avant-garde filmmakers, by addressing viewers directly and breaking the conventions of realism.[50]

Valdez discusses the audience reaction to *Zoot Suit*: "The fact that in 1978 . . . thousands of people were clamoring to get into this theatre to see a play, really spoke to the need . . . for people to see themselves, to reaffirm their own existence by seeing themselves reflected."[51]

HISTORICAL RECONSTRUCTION: THE BALLAD OF GREGORIO CORTEZ

Another example of film as an expression of historical reality is *The Ballad of Gregorio Cortez* (1982), directed by Robert M. Young. The film is based on Dr. Américo Paredes's 1958 historical study *With His Pistol in His Hand: A Border Ballad and Its Hero*.[52] Gregorio Cortez, played by Edward James Olmos, was a Mexican-American farmer wrongly accused of stealing a horse. Mistranslation due to prejudice results in the shooting death of Cortez's brother and the sheriff, and a manhunt in which Cortez is pursued to the Mexican border.[53] During the trial the issue of translation, which caused the problem, is raised but completely denied as a legitimate issue. The story is told from different points of view as in Akira Kurosawa's *Rashomon* (1950). The variation between the points of view suggests the limited objectivity of the persons recalling the events.

According to Olmos, in his Academy Visual History Interview, *The Ballad of Gregorio Cortez* is one of the first stories of an American hero of Mexican ancestry to be made for the big screen. He

talks about the director's aesthetic as one of authenticity—without romanticizing, glamorizing, exploiting, or manipulating the audience: "And that story was so incredibly done by Bob and . . . everybody involved, all of us, that the United States Historical Society has proclaimed it to be . . . totally accurate to the point where it could be used as a historical document."[54] Olmos attributes the authenticity to the use of actual locations and the way Young shot the film: "His psychological truth is so strong and understanding of where the psychological truth of the story is and where to place the camera."[55]

Olmos sees *The Ballad of Gregorio Cortez* as having contributed to the history of Latinos in the United States. Serving as a cornerstone of Chicano studies, the film allows people to experience United States history in a way never possible before.[56]

GREGORY NAVA: GIVING VOICE TO THE VOICELESS

Gregory Nava, in his Academy Visual History Interview, discusses some of his influences, particularly those with a non-European perspective. He likewise mentions the films of Satyajit Ray and Emilio Fernández, as well as Kurosawa's *Rashomon*

and *Seven Samurai* (1954): "when I saw *Ikiru* when I was in high school, I made a decision, that's what I want to do, I want to tell humanistic stories like *Ikiru*. I'm not Japanese, . . . didn't matter. I wept with, you know, the main character in *Ikiru*. I wept with Satyajit Ray and *The Apu Trilogy*. *The Bicycle Thief*. I'm not Italian in the post war, it didn't matter."[57]

He describes his film *El Norte* (1983) as this type of humanistic drama, which people anywhere in the world can identify with: "Okay, so I believe you tell the story of your village, you tell the story of the world, and you tell the truth. You tell it the way it

Far Left: Edward James Olmos in *Zoot Suit* (Luís Valdez, 1981). Center Left: Edward James Olmos in *The Ballad of Gregorio Cortez* (Robert M. Young, 1983).

Center Right: Still from *El Norte* (Gregory Nava, 1983). Far Right: Director and writer Gregory Nava speaks to a crowd in Mexico, undated.

truly is, and that meant it had to be about Rosa and Enrique. Their story, from their perspective, as they see the world."[58] The New Latin American Cinema gave voice to the voiceless; the images created were new to audiences not accustomed to seeing the faces of the common man on the screen. Nava comments, ". . . I had to put people in the shoes of Rosa and Enrique . . . . For all the voiceless voices. I wanted to give the voices to the shadows in the society."[59]

INFLUENCES GIVEN

IMPACT OF THE NEW LATIN AMERICAN CINEMA IN THE U.S.

The New Latin American Cinema has also had a profound influence on some filmmakers working in the U.S. Jonathan Demme, the Oscar-winning director of *Philadelphia* (1993) and *The Silence of the Lambs* (1991), credits Glauber Rocha's *Antonio das Mortes* as having a major impact on him. This film, about a legendary bounty hunter who sides with peasants in their struggle against a ruthless colonel, was banned by Brazil's military government. Rocha had to go into exile, similar to Sanjinés following *The Courage of the People*. Inspired by the film's style, Demme states: "Long before the invention of [the] Steadicam, and without the aid of cranes or dolly track, Glauber Rocha was . . . challenging the limits of just how much information, movement, theme, and suspense could be crammed into a single shot . . . *Antonio das Mortes* shocked me with the passion of its style and performances, thrilled me with the excitement of this new [to] me kind of cinema."[60]

Another Oscar-winning director, Martin Scorsese, has spoken of the impact Rocha's work had on his films *Mean Streets* (1973) and *Raging Bull* (1980). He describes seeing the Cinema Novo series at the Museum of Modern Art: "I think it was 1969, 1970, and I saw there *Terra em transe* (*Land in Anguish*) . . . *Land in Anguish* was very, very

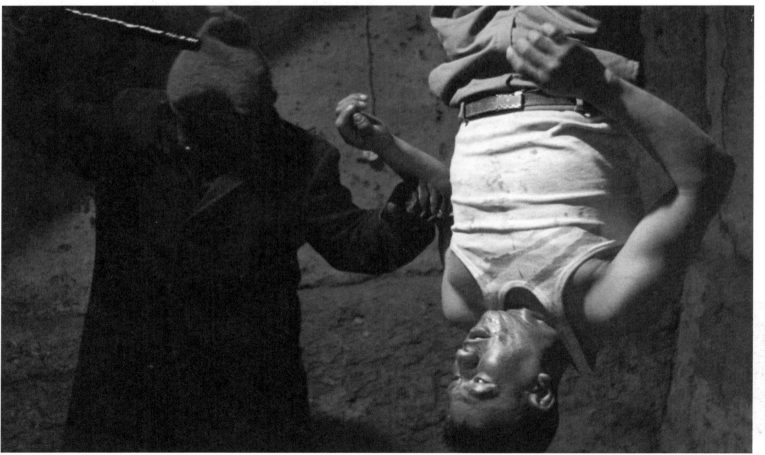

strong. I'd never seen anything quite like the combination of styles and, quite honestly, just the humanity and the passion of the film was so powerful. So when *Antonio das Mortes* opened at the Bleecker Street Cinema, and I saw the name Rocha, I went immediately to see this . . . At that time, every day—maybe I exaggerate—every three days, there was a new masterpiece, from Italy, from France, from Japan, from everywhere, I mean, it was all over. All of a sudden *Antonio das Mortes* comes onto the screen and wipes them all away."[61] In referring to *Antonio das Mortes*, Scorsese also addresses the role of the artist in creating awareness: "It's fresh, it's new, it doesn't cater to the tastes at the box office . . . this punches you in the face and wakes you up, opens your eyes, and that is what we need today more than ever."[62]

LATIN AMERICAN FILMS CONTINUE EXPLORING THEMES OF SOCIAL CONSCIOUSNESS

Among contemporary Latin American filmmakers who continue to be influenced by the Cinema Novo films of the 1960s is Walter Salles. His *Centro do Brasil* (*Central Station*, 1998) uses stark social realism to show an embittered woman who rediscovers faith in humanity on a journey to reunite a young boy with his father. In *Diários de motocicleta* (*The Motorcycle Diaries*, 2004), the major themes are "the value of friendship and the need for charity, hospitality, and dignity, lacking in an unjust society."[63] In both of these films, Salles also uses non-professional actors and what he refers to as "miracles of improvisation." *Central Station* includes footage of non-actors improvising as they dictate their letters to the protagonist. *The Motorcycle Diaries* uses unscripted, improvised interactions with people whom the protagonists, Ernesto and Alberto, meet along the way.[64]

Contemporary Latin American filmmakers also draw on many of the same influences as the New Latin American Cinema movement. In his Academy Visual History Interview, Alfonso Cuarón mentions that his mother took him to film clubs in Mexico City where he saw films by directors such as Kurosawa. He lists other influences: "*The Bicycle Thief*, which was fundamental in my childhood when I saw it for the first time, . . . and the early Godard was a very big influence for *Y tu mamá también*."[65] Cuarón, along with fellow directors from Mexico, Alejandro G. Iñárritu and Guillermo del Toro, was also influenced by international filmmakers such as Arturo Ripstein,

Federico Fellini, Michelangelo Antonioni, Steven Spielberg, Walter Hill, and Don Siegel.[66]

As with the New Latin American Cinema movement, these threads of inspiration crisscross the planet. Thus, some contemporary Latin American filmmakers express a desire to transcend borders. Cuarón states: "Human beings are born human, and only later some bureaucrats give them passports."[67]

Left: Production still of *El coraje del pueblo* (*The Courage of the People*, Jorge Sanjinés, 1971).

Right: Gael García Bernal and Rodrigo de la Serna in *Diários de motocicleta* (*The Motorcycle Diaries*, Walter Salles, 2004).

Guillermo del Toro echoes this desire to transcend borders: "Growing up as young filmmakers, we felt there should be no borders that define who we are, but there should be roots that define who we are. The difference is that borders confine you, roots nurture you."[68]

LA/LA GOING FORWARD

What will be the effect of the ongoing connections between Los Angeles and Latin America in the coming years? In his Academy Visual History Interview, Luís Valdez talks about U.S. history and the need to tell the story from viewpoints that challenge the "official story"concerning Western expansion, the history of California, and the Alamo. As a filmmaker, he sees this need as an opportunity: "I think that history is a living thing that can be reassessed and recalibrated with each generation . . . I'm not satisfied to say that today's films are as far as it goes . . . We need to move further."[69]

Jorge Sanjinés set out to use cinema not only to express historical reality but also to change history: "In Bolivia we're trying to make films that reflect the culture of the people, the culture of this country's suffering and exploited majority—the majority, which will one day be the true owners of their country when they gain political power. But to address oneself to this majority with the kind of political cinema we produce implies the development of a language appropriate to the vision this majority has of their reality."[70] Sanjinés' vision of indigenous empowerment became a reality in 2005 when, after 500 years of Spanish cultural dominance, the indigenous cultural majority democratically elected Bolivia's first indigenous president, Evo Morales Ayma.

Digital technology will likely continue to foster the development of indigenous cinema. Using this technology, Guatemalan director Jayro Bustamante made his first feature film *Ixcanul* (*Volcano*, 2015) about the life of a Mayan girl. Similar in approach to the New Latin American Cinema of the 1960s, the characters use their own language, Kaqchikel. In 2015, *Ixcanul* received the Alfred Bauer Prize at the Berlin International Film Festival.[71]

Colombia's first Academy Award nomination came in 2016 in the Foreign Language Film category with Ciro Guerra's film *El abrazo de la serpiente* (*Embrace of the Serpent*, 2015), which tells a story from an indigenous point of view. Guerra believes that is something Latin American directors can achieve: "The stories of the explorers have been told. What we can do is turn history on its head, give another perspective."[72]

JOSÉ SÁNCHEZ-H.

Professor, Film and Electronic Arts Department,
California State University, Long Beach

Dr. Sánchez-H. is a filmmaker and author of the book *The Art and Politics of Bolivian Cinema*, nominated for a Theatre Library Association Award. His ongoing research about Latin American cinema includes his collaboration on film preservation with the Academy Film Archive and the Los Angeles Latino International Film Festival, and his written contributions to the *International Film Guide*. He is the recipient of the Distinguished Faculty Scholarly and Creative Activities Award, the Spirit of Moondance Award, and the CSU Rosebud Award for achievement in media arts and education. Sánchez-H. co-authored the feature screenplay *La Paz*, a semifinalist in the Academy's Fellowship in Screenwriting Competition. His films have aired on Sundance Channel and have screened at international film festivals in Europe and the Americas. He holds a Ph.D. in Radio, TV and Film from the University of Michigan.

Left: Nilbio Torres in *El abrazo de la serpiente* (*Embrace of the Serpent*, Ciro Guerra, 2015).

NOTES

1. Nancy Caro Hollander, *Uprooted Minds: Surviving the Politics of Terror in the Americas* (New York: Routledge, 2010), 34.

2. Jorge Ruffinelli, "The Battle of Chile,"in *The Cinema of Latin America,* ed. Alberto Elena and Marina Díaz López (London: Wallflower Press, 2003), 151.

3. José Sánchez-H., *The Art and Politics of Bolivian Cinema* (Lanham, MD: Scarecrow Press, 1999), 77–78.

4. B. Ruby Rich, "An/Other View of Latin American Cinema," in *New Latin American Cinema vol. 1*, ed. Michael T. Martin (Detroit: Wayne State University Press, 1997), 277.

5. Robert Phillip Kolker, *The Altering Eye* (Oxford: Oxford University Press, 1983), 190.

6. Jorge Sanjinés, "Problems of Form and Content in Revolutionary Cinema," in *New Latin American Cinema vol. 1*, ed. Michael T. Martin (Detroit: Wayne State University Press, 1997), 63.

7. Mariano Mestman and Maria Luisa Ortega, "Grierson and Latin America: Encounters, Dialogues and Legacies," in *The Grierson Effect: Tracing Documentary's International Movement*, ed. Zoë Druick and Deane Williams (London: BFI, 2014), 223.

8. Zuzana M. Pick, *The New Latin American Cinema: A Continental Project* (Austin: University of Texas Press, 1993), 16.

9. Mestman and Ortega, "Grierson and Latin America," 224.

10. Julianne Burton, *Cinema and Social Change in Latin America: Conversations with Filmmakers* (Austin: University of Texas Press, 1986), 18.

11. Academy Visual History with Nelson Pereira dos Santos, interviewed by Mateus Araujo in Rio de Janeiro, March 22, 2016.

12. Mestman and Ortega, "Grierson and Latin America," 233.

13. Charles Ramirez Berg, "The Cinematic Invention of Mexico: The Poetics and Politics of the Fernández-Figueroa Style," in *The Mexican Cinema Project*, ed. Chon Noriega and Steven Ricci (UCLA Film and Television Archive, 1994), 17.

14. Juan Pablo Avila-Ramírez, "Jorge Ruiz: persona fundamental en la historia del cine boliviano," *La Revista*, Edición N° 33, La Paz (2009).

15. John King, *Magical Reels: A History of Cinema in Latin America*, 2nd ed. (London: Verso, 2000), 190.

16. José Antonio Valdivia, *Testigo de la realidad: Jorge Ruiz, memorias del cine documental boliviano* (La Paz: Centro de Información para el Desarrollo-CID, 1998).

17. Ibid.

18. Ibid.

19. Sánchez-H., *The Art and Politics of Bolivian Cinema*, 77.

20. Jorge Sanjinés's Ukamau Group, *Teoría y Práctica de un cine junto al pueblo* (Mexico: Siglo XXI, 1979), 97–98.

21. John Hess, "Neo-realism and New Latin American Cinema: Bicycle Thieves and Blood of the Condor," in *Mediating Two Worlds* (London: British Film Institute, 1993), 114.

22. Sánchez-H., *The Art and Politics of Bolivian Cinema*, 77.

23. Julianne Burton, "Film Artisans and Film Industries in Latin America, 1956-1980," in *New Latin American Cinema* vol. 1, ed. Michael T. Martin (Detroit: Wayne State University Press, 1997), 160.

24. Pick, *The New Latin American Cinema: A Continental Project*, 16.

25. John King, "Andean Images," in *New Latin American Cinema* vol. 2, ed. Michael T. Martin (Detroit: Wayne State University Press, 1997), 490.

26. King, *Magical Reels*, 197.

27. Leonardo Garcia-Pabón, "The Clandestine Nation: Indigenism and National Subjects of Bolivia in the Films of Jorge Sanjinés," trans. Maura Furfey *Jump Cut 44* (Fall 2001): 2, accessed June 30, 2016, doi: http://www.ejumpcut.org/archive/jc44.2001/garcia/garciaforsite.html

28. Chon Noriega, "Imagined Borders: Locating Chicano Cinema in America/América," in *The Ethnic Eye: Latino Media Arts*, ed. Chon Noriega (Minneapolis: University of Minnesota Press, 1996), 15.

29. Academy Visual History with Luís Valdez, interviewed by Lourdes Portillo in San Juan Bautista, June 8, 2014.

30. Noriega, "Imagined Borders," 16.

31. Ibid.

32. Alfredo Guevara, "Palabras de Presentación," in *23 Festival Internacional del Nuevo Cine Latinoamericano* (La Habana: Ediciones Portón Caribe S.A. , 2001), 6–7.

33. Noriega, "Imagined Borders," 4, 18.

34. *A Decade Under the Influence*, directed by Ted Demme and Richard LaGravenese (2003; USA: Independent Film Channel, 2003), DVD.

35. Dina Nascetti, "The Courage of the People: An Interview with Jorge Sanjinés," *Cineaste* Vol. 5, No. 2, Spring 1972, 20.

36. Noriega, "Imagined Borders," 8–10.

37. Noriega, "Imagined Borders," Ibid., 4–5.

38. Academy Visual History with Luís Valdez, interviewed by Lourdes Portillo in San Juan Bautista, June 8, 2014.

39. Noriega, "Imagined Borders," 7.

40. Rosa-Linda Fregoso, *The Bronze Screen* (Minneapolis: University of Minnesota Press, 1993), 3.

41. Ibid., 7.

42. Ibid., 10.

43. Ibid., 10.

44. Noriega, "Imagined Borders," 7.

45. Academy Visual History with Luís Valdez, interviewed by Lourdes Portillo in San Juan Bautista, June 8, 2014.

46. Ibid.

47. Mario Barrera, "Story in Latino Feature Films," in *Chicanos and Film*, ed. Chon Noriega (New York: Garland Publishing, Inc., 1992), 26.

48. Fregoso, *The Bronze Screen*, 24.

49. Barrera, "Story in Latino Feature Films," 262–263.

50. Fregoso, *The Bronze Screen*, 24.

51. Academy Visual History with Luís Valdez, interviewed by Lourdes Portillo in San Juan Bautista, June 8, 2014.

52. Markus Heide, "From Zorro to Jennifer Lopez: US-Latino History and Film for the EFL-Classroom." *American Studies Journal* 51 (2008): 12, accessed June 30, 2016, doi: http://www.asjournal.org/51-2008/from-zorro-to-jennifer-lopez/

53. Academy Visual History with Edward James Olmos, interviewed by Lourdes Portillo in Encino, May 15, 2014.

54. Ibid.

55. Ibid.

56. Ibid.

57. Academy Visual History with Gregory Nava, interviewed by Lourdes Portillo in Beverly Hills, June 16, 2015.

58. Ibid.

59. Ibid.

60. Rob Edelman, "Filmmakers, actors, reveal movies that had major impact on them," *The Daily Gazette*, December 30, 1995, accessed May 27, 2016, https://news.google.com/newspapers?nid=1957&dat=19951230&id=d3lGAAA AIBAJ&sjid=HekMAAAAIBAJ&pg=1063,6934569&hl=en

61. *Scorsese on Rocha* 1, YouTube video, 14:10, posted by "arthur4350," November 8, 2010, https://www.youtube.com/watch?v=V6U0BHaptg62. *Scorsese on Rocha* 2, YouTube video, 14:45, posted by "arthur4350," November 8, 2010, https://www.youtube.com/watch?v=TPuL9pJZEVA

63. Claire Williams, "Los diarios de motocicleta as Pan-American Travelogue," in *Contemporary Latin American Cinema*, ed. Deborah Shaw (Lanham: Rowman & Littlefield Publishers, Inc., 2007), 15–16.

64. Ibid., 13.

65. Academy Visual History with Alfonso Cuarón, interviewed by Lourdes Portillo in London, February 11, 2016.

66. Reed Johnson, "A bond beyond borders," *Los Angeles Times*, October 1, 2006, accessed May 27, 2016, http://www.latimes.com/la-fg-inarritu-story.html

67. Academy Visual History with Alfonso Cuarón, interviewed by Lourdes Portillo in London, February 11, 2016.

68. Johnson, "A bond beyond borders."

69. Academy Visual History with Luís Valdez, interviewed by Lourdes Portillo in San Juan Bautista, June 8, 2014.

70. *New Cinema of Latin America*, Part 2, The Long Road, DVD, directed by Michael Chanan (1985; UK: Channel Four, 1985).

71. Jeffrey Fleishman, and Carolina A. Miranda, "How foreign directors are flipping the script on Hollywood story ideas," *Los Angeles Times*, February 19, 2016, accessed May 27, 2016, http://www.latimes.com/entertainment/la-ca-mn-foreign-directors-20160221-html- htmlstory.html

72. Ibid.

LATINO FILMMAKERS
AS MULTICULTURAL
EDUCATORS

BY: CARLOS E. CORTÉS

Movies teach. Such teaching occurs whether or not filmmakers actually view themselves as educators. Framed another way, audiences often learn from movies—feature films as well as documentaries—regardless of the viewer's awareness or the filmmaker's conscious intentions.

For the past forty years I have been analyzing this phenomenon, focusing on the relationship between mass media and audience learning about diversity. My major concern has been the process by which media have influenced multicultural perceptions of self and others. This research became the basis for my book, *The Children Are Watching: How the Media Teach about Diversity*.[1]

One issue addressed in the book—particularly in Chapter 3, "Mediamakers as Multicultural Curriculum Developers"—was the extent to which media people, including filmmakers, have been conscious that they have functioned as de facto educators: that their media products may have influenced audience multicultural learning. For the Academy of Motion Picture Arts and Sciences' *Pacific Standard Time: LA/LA* project, I examine this topic by drawing upon a rich, newly-created source of evidence: The Academy's Visual History Interviews with a number of U.S. Latino filmmakers, including Mexican Americans Gregory Nava, Edward James Olmos, and Luís Valdez.

Based on my analysis of those interviews, I concluded that, indeed, these three filmmakers have been acutely aware of their pedagogical function. That is, they attempted to use their feature films to try to teach, thereby influencing the public image of Latinos. Moreover, beyond this general consciousness, at different times they have had very specific ideas about the nature of their

pedagogical roles. The interviews reveal that at self-identified moments—possibly even continuously throughout their filmmaking (and theatrical) careers—these three have tended to view themselves more specifically as revisionist historians, intercultural anthropologists, civic values inculcators, and educational reformers.

ESTABLISHING THE CONTEXT

Teaching is clearly inherent in the process of making documentary and so-called "educational" films. However, some might be surprised by the pedagogical awareness of many involved in making movies sometimes classified as entertainment, such as feature films. Contributors to feature films—including directors, producers, writers, and actors—have often been acutely aware of their public teaching role, the fact that they are creating a media curriculum that operates parallel to the school curriculum.

In the 1970s I began using the term, "the societal curriculum," to encapsulate the chaotic informal non-school curriculum involving such "teachers" as families, peers, communities, social organizations, religious institutions, and media.[2] Within that societal curriculum, the media, including feature motion pictures, play a particularly powerful role.

In the case of Latinos, the media—until recently, the traditional mass media—may have historically played a more significant image-creating curricular role than schools themselves. This was certainly true until at least the 1970s. Until then, most K-12 textbooks and school curricula exhibited only sporadic attention to Latinos. At best, students might have encountered an elementary school unit on California missions, a mention of the Battle of the

Alamo, a brief discussion of the annexation of one-third of Mexico after the 1846-1848 U.S.-Mexican War, or an occasional reference to Mexican immigration. But until the 1970s, U.S. Latinos had little textbook presence in pre-college curricula, and even today they have relatively limited visibility. As a result, until recently the media held a virtual monopoly on the creation of the Latino public image.

Because of the popularity of movies and their well-documented ability to influence public perceptions, numerous scholars of the Latino experience have taken an interest in the Latino image in film.[3] Their research has clearly demonstrated the long tradition of negative Latino movie depictions stretching back to the "greaser" films of the early silent era, such as *The Greaser's Gauntlet* (D.W. Griffith, 1908) and *Guns and Greasers* (Lawrence Semon, 1918).[4]

However, in the 1970s there arose a generation of activist Latino filmmakers—including Edward James Olmos, Luís Valdez, and Gregory Nava—who would begin challenging these images. The arrival of that generation raises an important set of questions. How aware were these Latino filmmakers of the fact that they were combating a historically grounded U.S. moviemaking tradition? How conscious were they that they were creating a filmic counter-curriculum on Latinos? In what respects did this socio-historical consciousness influence their filmmaking trajectories? The Academy Visual History Interviews provide revealing insights for considering these questions.

In analyzing the project's lengthy interviews with these three filmmakers, I focused on one central question: in what respects do these interviews

Pervious Page: Director
Luis Valdez during production
of La Bamba (1987).
Left: Director and writer
Gregory Nava on set, undated.
Right: Portrait of Edward
James Olmos, undated.

reveal the existence of a multicultural pedagogical consciousness? Those interviews provide a clear and compelling answer. These filmmakers *did* view themselves as educators, but not just as educators writ large. They often viewed themselves as very specific types of teachers.

Although the creation of analytical categories can unwittingly distort through oversimplification, it can also provide a framework for focusing the evidence. Therefore, heeding Albert Einstein's advice that analysts should make everything "as simple as possible, but not simpler" and using these interviews as my source, I teased out four types of multicultural pedagogical consciousness that these three Latino filmmakers revealed through their personal narratives. At different times and in the making of various films, those filmmakers appeared to view themselves as:

1) Revisionist historians—challenging the long-extant trajectory of traditional feature film depictions of Latinos when presenting the U.S. past.

2) Intercultural anthropologists—contending with the way that Latino culture has been portrayed in traditional feature films and exploring Latino social and cultural practices in their own filmmaking.

3) Civic values inculcators—attempting to convey constructive civic norms and values, particularly when it came to influencing the values and behavior of Latino youth.

4) Educational reformers—examining the education of young Latinos, indicating reformist possibilities, and considering the personal educational needs of Latinos.

LATINO FILMMAKERS AS REVISIONIST HISTORIANS

Historical thinking has had a powerful influence on these three Latino filmmakers, particularly regarding their connection to their Mexican heritage. Discussing his film *My Family* (*Mi familia*, 1995), Gregory Nava muses,

> But the film that I made that really for me as the quintessential film about Los Angeles and the Latino experience in Los Angeles was my film, Mi familia/ My Family . . . I wanted to make a film in which the family and the city become one, and they grow together and you see the changes through three generations of this city . . . the Latino experience is at the heart of what this city is, and this is what the film Mi Familia shows.[5]

Luís Valdez recalls his viewing experience as a twelve-year-old of the 1952 film *Viva Zapata!* (Elia Kazan, 1952) starring Marlon Brando as the famed Mexican revolutionary, and considers it to be a life-altering event. "I knew about Pancho Villa. I never knew about Emiliano Zapata until I saw Brando portray Emiliano Zapata. I don't have the specifics. But it was enough to really plant the seed."[6] Years later Valdez would use Zapata's revolutionary proclamation "El Plan de Ayala" as a model for his own "El Plan de Delano," which was created as an ideological basis for César Chávez' organizing of agricultural workers and his 1966 300-mile protest march from Delano to Sacramento.

Still from *My Family* (*Mi familia*, Gregory Nava, 1995).

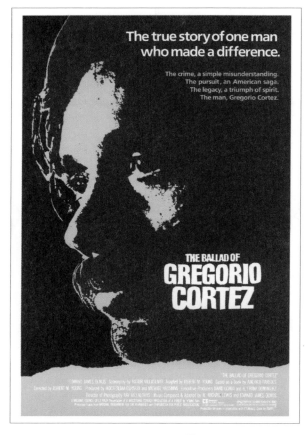

Valdez engaged in considerable historical research for his projects. For his play and later film, *Zoot Suit* (1981), Valdez conducted extensive oral history interviewing with those involved in seminal World War II-era Los Angeles events: the Zoot Suit riots; the Sleepy Lagoon affair; and the subsequent trials. Later, for *La Bamba* (1987), his biographical exploration of Chicano singer Ritchie Valens (née Richard Valenzuela), one of Valdez's challenges was to recreate the dirt streets of Pacoima in which Valenzuela grew up.

As Edward James Olmos recounts, "no single artist has influenced me more in my lifetime than Paul Muni did when I saw him perform as Benito Juárez."[7] This Jewish American actor's portrayal of the legendary mid-nineteenth-century Mexican president in *Juarez* (William Dieterle, 1939) appears to have kindled a historical consciousness that remained with Olmos as he himself engaged in teaching about the U.S. Latino experience through film.

This Latino-oriented historical consciousness deeply infused Olmos' work with director Robert M. Young in the making of the film *The Ballad of Gregorio Cortez* (1982), a film Olmos refers to as "the most fulfilling piece of work I've ever been involved with."[8] The film, based on Américo Paredes' classic study, "*With His Pistol in His Hand:*" *A Border Ballad and Its Hero*,[9] recounts the story of a fabled South Texas manhunt for Cortez, a Chicano who fled from a shoot-out sparked by a translation error during a conversation between the Spanish-speaking Cortez and an English-speaking sheriff.

In creating the script and selecting film sites, Olmos and Young scoured locations in Gonzales, Texas, where the original shoot-out occurred, and studied stacks of court transcripts. Olmos proudly refers to the film as "the most authentic western ever made in American history," which "allowed people to experience the United States of America in a way they had never experienced it before in history of film."[10]

LATINO FILMMAKERS AS INTERCULTURAL ANTHROPOLOGISTS

Valdez discusses the process of becoming liberated from the powerful anthropological lesson taught by the first feature film he ever saw, the 1936 rendition of James Fenimore Cooper's novel *The Last of the Mohicans* (George B. Seitz, 1936). Recalling the scene of a white man being burned at the stake, Valdez notes, "And I thought those Indians were terrible. Not realizing that I was an Indian myself. And I was really afraid of my own people, in that regard. So of course I would completely identify with the white people."[11]

When it came to *Zoot Suit,* both Valdez and Olmos appear to have become acutely aware of their roles as intercultural anthropologists. In writing the play, Valdez drew heavily from personal cultural experience.

> And so when I came up and was doing the conceptual work for Zoot Suit, and decided to take on the pachuco, I was really tapping into my childhood memories. And among those, one of the figures that contributed to that statuesque pachuco in the play is CC [César Chávez], my cousin Billy, and all the pachucos that I met, you know. They seemed like giants to me. And so the only way that I could represent them is almost as a mythological figure.[12]

Olmos quickly connected with Valdez's anthropological conception. When asked to audition for the iconic role of El Pachuco, Olmos drew upon his street experience. He recognized El Pachuco both as the Greek chorus of the play and as the embodiment of what he had grown up with in East Los Angeles. Olmos recalls looking at the single page of dialogue for his audition :

> This is not Spanish. This is the stuff I heard on the street in front of my house, done by

*the home boys . . . The way the local kids
used to talk . . . I walked in like the chucos
that I used to see in the corner, man, they
had an attitude, they wore their pride . . . So
I walked into the reading of the thing with
an attitude, boom.*[13]

Nava, too, drew upon personal cultural experience in making his film *El Norte* (1983), the dramatic story of two Guatemalan siblings who flee from their home country, manage to traverse obstacles within Mexico, and finally succeed in entering the United States, where they each achieve minor successes before ultimately encountering personal tragedy.

*You know it was my story really, from the
world. Because I've seen people from
when I was a little boy. Like you saw in
the film. Crossing from Tijuana, from the
horrible ciudades perdidas, these lost cities of cardboard and poverty that exist in
Tijuana, the contrast between Tijuana and
San Diego is so graphic, right. And I saw
this from when I was a child.*[14]

Anthropological thinking, particularly an immersion in Mesoamerican spiritual beliefs and traditions, became central to Nava as he developed *El Norte*. "And it was important to me that you have these two lead roles, Rosa and Enrique, this duality. Because . . . all pre-Columbian, Mesoamerican mythology, it's always twin heroes . . . Rosa dies, and she is associated with the lunar imagery, and Enrique with the solar imagery." [15] Drawing upon the "underworld" theme of Mesoamerican mythology, Nava created *El Norte* (the United States) as his filmic underworld.

Olmos's anthropological thinking also appears to have informed his participation in the making

Left: Poster from
The Ballad of Gregorio Cortez
(Robert Young, 1983).
Right: Edward James Olmos in
Zoot Suit (Luís Valdez, 1981).

of Ridley Scott's film, *Blade Runner* (1982). Olmos recalls that, in his first meeting with Scott, he asserted that, "I want my character to know where he comes from"[16] and proceeded to lay out his character's multicultural genealogy. In preparing for the role, Olmos studied at Berlitz to perfect the intercultural nature of his dialogue, which he used to suggest to audiences the possible nature of communication in a futuristic multiethnic Los Angeles.[17]

Valdez's quest for cultural fidelity, particularly regarding Latinos, extended into his relationship with other filmmakers. He recounts an interaction with director Michael Schultz, who asked him to

read the script for the Richard Pryor film, *Which Way Is Up?* (1977). Valdez told him bluntly: "The rest of the script is funny . . . But this part about the farm workers is really bad."[18] To which Schultz responded by hiring Valdez to rewrite some of the scenes.

LATINO FILMMAKERS AS CIVIC VALUES INCULCATORS

One fact that arises from the Academy Visual History Interviews is that these three Latino filmmakers had an awareness that at times they were using their movies to inculcate civic values. Such was the case of Olmos' film *American Me* (1992), which

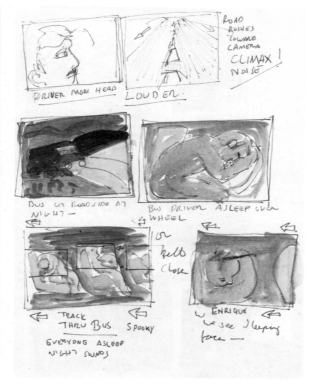

featured Olmos as a Mexican Mafia drug lord. This film, which served as Olmos's feature film directorial debut, included scenes shot in Folsom Prison.

While Olmos admits that *American Me* may be "too dark" he takes pride in what the film has done to help young kids, particularly young Latinos, develop more constructive civic values. "It has saved more

kids than anything we've ever done. It allows you to experience inside of that world and then you have a choice. You have a real, honest choice . . . It'll either help you become a better soldier or help you to stay away from having to go through that journey 'cause you've already experienced it."[19]

Nava's original decision to make *El Norte* came from his reaction to a *Los Angeles Times* story depicting the growth of the city's Latino population as a threat to the broader community. In that film, Nava provides a type of civics counter-lesson by humanizing Latino immigration. As he recounted the impetus for the film, Nava explained,

> *Somebody should make a movie about . . . the shadows that are in our city. Mowing all the lawns . . . taking care of the babies . . . someone should make a movie to give a heart and soul to the shadows that are pervading the city. To give voice to the voiceless . . . . I thought, if I don't make this movie, nobody is going to make this movie . . . . And I started, the very next day, to write the script to* El Norte.[20]

Valdez, too, saw the importance of civic values in what he created. He viewed *Zoot Suit* as

> *a story about the evolution of social justice . . . . The case is really one about questioning racism. The mass trial of the 22 members of the 38th Street gang was a reflex that reflected the racism of Los Angeles. And the Sleepy Lagoon case, the defense committee, and eventually the overturning of the guilty pleas on appeal, I think is a reaffirmation of American values in a sense that social justice is possible.[21]*

LATINO FILMMAKERS AS EDUCATIONAL REFORMERS

At times these three filmmakers have used movies to consciously address the education of Latino youth. Such was the experience of Olmos with the film, *Stand and Deliver* (Ramón Menéndez, 1987), about the renowned Bolivian American mathematics teacher, Jaime Escalante, and his success in helping Los Angeles Latino high school students pass the Advanced Placement calculus examination. Olmos had met Escalante at an awards ceremony of the National Association for the Advancement of Colored People and interviewed him at length in preparing the script.

As much as Olmos takes pride in the film, he takes additional satisfaction in the fact that teachers use it in their classrooms. Yet, as Olmos muses, "I don't know how a teacher could show that movie and then get up and start trying to teach a class after the whole class saw Jaime Escalante teach."[22]

Reflecting on the thousands of Latinos who saw his play (later film) *Zoot Suit*, Valdez implicitly

Far Left: Edward James Olmos in *Blade Runner* (Ridley Scott, 1982). Middle Left: Storyboards for *El Norte* (1983) from the personal notebooks of Gregory Nava.

Center Left: Costume illustration by Julian Mendoza for *American Me* for Edward James Olmos, 1992. Right: Edward James Olmos and Jaime Escalante during production of *Stand and Deliver* (Ramón Menéndez, 1988).

recognizes the limited Latino curricular presence, be it in the school curriculum or in the motion picture curriculum. He points to "the pressing need for people to see themselves, to reaffirm their own existence by seeing themselves reflected."[23]

Nava indicates comparable thinking about the Latino image and the educational importance of Latino role models in his making of *Selena* (1997), the biographical story of fabled Tejana singer Selena Quintanilla-Pérez. As he recounts, ". . . I met these two little girls, they were Latina . . . and they had Selena t-shirts. And I asked them, 'Why do you love Selena?' And they said to me, 'Because she looks like us.' . . . And so I thought, I want to make this movie for these girls."[24]

BEYOND LATINIDAD

All three of these filmmakers have been involved in discovering, resurrecting, and transforming Latino stories into film. In doing so, they have challenged the generally overlooked and often disrespected place of Latinos in the informal motion picture curriculum on America. They have also championed the importance of establishing Latinos as more than merely American ethnics. In the process they appear to be striving for even more ambitious public teaching goals: the assertion of Latinos as a vital part of the broader United States historical trajectory and socio-cultural fabric; and the celebrating of the universal humanity inherent to Latino stories.

Recalling the creation of *Zoot Suit*, Valdez opines:

The whole pachuco experience is about cultural fusion it seems to me. Because if you're going to talk Zoot Suit, you have to talk about its roots in the African American

experience as well . . . And it became a style then that young people picked up being emblematic of their American identity. And because it does come from so many sources. It's an expression of American cultural fusion, that the American identity is a fusion of different cultures.[25]

An effort to embed Latinos within the larger picture of American diversity also infuses Nava's documentary film *American Tapestry* (2000). Beyond this, he expresses the hope that "someday we reach a point where people can see my films . . . and see also what the more universal themes are that we're

talking about in our films, and not just these cultural things, because they are so important in a society which obviously we have diversity issues and all kinds of issues."[26]

As Olmos told Lourdes Portillo in his Academy Visual History Interview, "The stories that we've been able to create, I think, are stories that speak to the humanness of all of us, no matter the culture. It resonates inside of humanity . . . . I think in a hundred years the films that I've made will be more poignant than they are today."[27]

CREATING A LATINO FILM VISION

As the Academy's Oral History Project reveal, these three Latino filmmakers—Luís Valdez, Gregory Nava, and Edward James Olmos—share a robust vision of their place within the long trajectory of the motion picture curriculum on Latinos. All three have operated with a deep awareness of how Latinos—particularly Mexican Americans—have traditionally been either omitted from or pilloried by U.S. media, especially feature films. Moreover, their interviews exude a commitment to challenging that trajectory.

But beyond this, the three filmmakers appear to share a broader vision. While proud of exposing Americans to Latino stories, they view themselves not simply as making ethnic films. Rather all three see their Latino narratives as quintessentially American stories that shine a new light on the trajectory of U.S. history and the socio-cultural complexity of the contemporary American scene. Moreover, they take pride in the idea that their stories contain a sense of universality, which allows their Latino narratives to reach across ethnic and national barriers and address fundamental dilemmas of a morally complex world.

DR. CARLOS CORTÉS

Professor Emeritus of History,
University of California, Riverside

Dr. Cortés is a prominent writer-lecturer specializing in diversity, including its role in the media. He addressed this in his book, *The Children Are Watching: How the Media Teach about Diversity* (Teachers College Press, 2000). His most recent books are his memoir, *Rose Hill: An Intermarriage before Its Time* (Heyday, 2012) and a book of poetry, *Fourth Quarter: Reflections of a Cranky Old Man* (Bad Knee Press, 2016). He also edited the four-volume *Multicultural America: A Multimedia Encyclopedia* (Sage, 2013). Cortés has won numerous awards, including the NAACP Image Award, NASPA's Outstanding Contribution to Higher Education Award, ASTD's National Multicultural Trainer of the Year Award, the California Association for Bilingual Education's Inspiration Award, and the California Council for the Humanities' Distinguished California Humanist Award. He continues to serve as a consultant to government agencies, educational institutions, mass media, private businesses, and non-profits throughout the United States, Europe, Asia, Latin America, and Australia.

Left: Jennifer Lopez in *Selena*
(Gregory Nava, 1997).

NOTES

1. Carlos E. Cortés, *The Children Are Watching: How the Media Teach about Diversity* (New York: Teachers College Press, 2000).

2. Carlos E. Cortés, "The Societal Curriculum and the School Curriculum: Allies or Antagonists?," *Educational Leadership* XXXVI 7 (April, 1979): 475-480.

3. Chon A. Noriega, ed., *Chicanos and Film: Representation and Resistance* (Minneapolis: University of Minnesota Press, 1992).

4. Blaine Lamb, "The Convenient Villain: The Early Cinema Views the Mexican-American," *Journal of the West* XIV 4 (October, 1975): 80-81.

5. Academy Visual History with Gregory Nava, interviewed by Ellen Harrington in Beverly Hills, March 9, 2016.

6. Academy Visual History with Luís Valdez, interviewed by Lourdes Portillo in San Juan Bautista, June 8, 2014.

7. Academy Visual History with Edward James Olmos, interviewed by Lourdes Portillo in Encino, May 15, 2014.

8. Ibid.

9. Américo Paredes, *"With His Pistol in His Hand:" A Border Ballad and Its Hero* (Austin: University of Texas Press, 1958).

10. Academy Visual History with Edward James Olmos, interviewed by Lourdes Portillo in Encino, May 15, 2014.

11. Academy Visual History with Luís Valdez, interviewed by Lourdes Portillo in San Juan Bautista, June 8, 2014.

12. Ibid.

13. Academy Visual History with Edward James Olmos, interviewed by Lourdes Portillo in Encino, May 15, 2014.

14. Academy Visual History with Gregory Nava, interviewed by Lourdes Portillo in Beverly Hills, June 16, 2015.

15. Ibid.

16. Academy Visual History with Edward James Olmos, interviewed by Lourdes Portillo in Encino, May 15, 2014.

17. Ibid.

18. Academy Visual History with Luís Valdez, interviewed by Lourdes Portillo in San Juan Bautista, June 8, 2014.

19. Academy Visual History with Edward James Olmos, interviewed by Lourdes Portillo in Encino, May 15, 2014.

20. Academy Visual History with Gregory Nava, interviewed by Lourdes Portillo in Beverly Hills, June 16, 2015.

21. Academy Visual History with Luís Valdez, interviewed by Lourdes Portillo in San Juan Bautista, June 8, 2014.

22. Academy Visual History with Edward James Olmos, interviewed by Lourdes Portillo in Encino, May 15, 2014.

23. Academy Visual History with Luís Valdez, interviewed by Lourdes Portillo in San Juan Bautista, June 8, 2014.

24. Academy Visual History with Gregory Nava, interviewed by Lourdes Portillo in Beverly Hills, June 16, 2015.

25. Academy Visual History with Luís Valdez, interviewed by Lourdes Portillo in San Juan Bautista, June 8, 2014.

26. Academy Visual History with Gregory Nava, interviewed by Ellen Harrington in Beverly Hills, March 9, 2016.

27. Academy Visual History with Edward James Olmos, interviewed by Lourdes Portillo in Encino, May 15, 2014.

A CINEMA
OF HER OWN

BY: ROSA-LINDA FREGOSO

"Women filmmakers of my generation did contribute," María Novaro insists. "We opened up . . . a monolithic language expressed in movies being made by men . . . I feel that the country still needs to open itself up to its own [ethnic] diversity . . . but a beginning was to open itself up to feminine thinking."[2]

As I contemplate the role of U.S. Latinas and Latin American women in cinema, Mexican filmmaker María Novaro's discerning words suggest that it does matter who is behind the camera as director, writer, or cinematographer. But to what extent does gender diversity necessarily guarantee a female perspective? Does the inclusion of women in the film industry—and not just on the screen—result in a different kind of cinema? Novaro hints that making films from a woman's own perspective—the mode of expression that she calls "feminine thinking"—has made an appreciable difference in how audiences see the world, how we interpret reality, and the kind and quality of stories we see on screen.

Women's cinema—as a genre of films highlighting a female perspective—circulates largely in festivals and art house film circuits, rather than in commercial industry networks that, on a global scale, continue to be dominated by Hollywood franchises. According to the "Women in Independent Films" report, women account for twenty-eight percent of directors at film festivals compared with nine percent who worked on films at major Hollywood Studios during 2015.[3] The bulk of women-centered stories are told in documentary format, and feature films in Latin America are largely transnational co-productions financed by two or more nationally based production companies.

If, as film critic Alison Butler contends, "women's cinema is not 'at home' in any of the host of cinematic or national discourses it inhabits,"[4] her statement pertains to women's cinema in Latin America as well as in the United States, where only a handful of Latinas in the U.S. film industry have made feature films about women. As discouraging as this gender/racial disparity may be, it has not extinguished Latinas' desire to create "a cinema of her own."[5]

There is a difference between women making films from a gender perspective and women working in the industry. As their presence in cinema continues to expand, so too will our awareness of their impact on national and world film cultures. In the following pages I profile filmmakers interviewed as part of the Academy's *Pacific Standard Time: LA/LA* project, starting first with women whose works embody a female perspective in shaping a cinema of her own. This "cinema of her own" is neither monolithic nor one-dimensional. It reflects the diversity of women's stories, histories, cultures, and languages, as illustrated in the works of directors from Mexico and Argentina working on Spanish-language films in their respective countries; a Colombian-born director helming mostly English-language films in Los Angeles; and a Mexican-born Chicana documentarian based in San Francisco, filming in both languages. I end my essay by featuring two Mexican women working in other creative behind-the-scenes roles in the film industry.

MARÍA NOVARO

"When my sister and I wrote *Danzón* (1991),we explicitly said, 'It's going to be another women's movie, with a female point of view, from our way of seeing the world . . . but let's not let [the audience] realize it, or when they realize it, it's too late, they would already like it," María Novaro declares in her Academy Visual History Interview.[6]

Watching María Novaro's films, one feels as though the person behind the camera sees the world in a different way, creating what she calls "another way of framing life, another temporality, another relationship with details . . ."[7] She taps into "the feminine soul," what it is to be Mexican *and* woman in a "landscape so distinctly shaped by gender."[8]

Her early and most recent works—*Una isla rodeada de agua* (*An Island Surrounded by Water*, 1984) and *Las buenas hierbas* (*The Good Herbs*, 2011) are both melodramas exploring how abandonment or illness test the deep bonds between mothers and daughters. The intervening films illustrate Novaro's proclivity for creating women-centered dramas.

Once a single mother of three, Novaro populates her stories with kindred female characters whose lives are not dependent on men but on the emotional and spiritual bonds forged with other women. *Lola* (1988) tells the story of a single mother struggling to survive in the aftermath of the devastation caused by Mexico City's 1985 earthquake. Considered a cult feminist movie for its genuine and realistic portrayal of a far-from-perfect mother, *Lola* won four Silver Ariel awards[9] despite garnering negative reviews by male critics who berated its flawed image of Mexican motherhood.[10] As Novaro explains, "Their critiques were very moralistic. They were appalled by the depiction of an unobligated mother who did not take good care of her daughter, who drank beer and had boyfriends . . . Every one of the male critics was absolutely judgmental, as evident by the words of one critic: 'And that director, that woman, has the nerve to dedicate the movie to her own children.'"[11]

In her second feature film *Danzón*, Novaro portrays a middle-aged telephone operator and single

mother living in Mexico City, whose one passion is danzón—the refined ballroom dancing in which men lead but women are its prime figures. When Julia's dance partner Carmelo fails to appear at their weekly dance rendezvous, she travels to his hometown of Veracruz and wanders the streets searching for him, befriending a drag queen and finding erotic passion with a young man half her age.

Danzón was the first Mexican film in seventeen years to be invited to the Cannes Film Festival. Co-written with her sister Beatriz Novaro and shot by Guillermo García (son of famed novelist Gabriel García Márquez), the film's commercial and critical reception in Europe and the U.S. propelled Novaro's international career and profile as a filmmaker.

Novaro's sensibility was honed in the trenches of Mexico's feminist and student activism of the seventies, and her early start in Mexico's film industry. She first made documentaries with Colectivo Cine Mujer, a collective of leftist militant feminists who pioneered the women's film movement in Mexico. "It was then that I fell in love with the camera," she explains. "I fell in love with the Nagra . . . for sound recording . . . with the Moviola . . . for editing 16 mm . . . with all the tools for making cinema, so I decided to enroll in the CUEC,"[12] Mexico's first film school.[13]

The protected and idyllic environment of the CUEC—where forty percent of the students were women— was short-lived. "As soon as I started my professional career in 1984 . . . I confronted the STPC (filmworkers union), whose statute literally stated that 'women could not touch a camera . . . I could work as a director as long as I did not hire women," Novaro explains.[14] Determined to hire a female crew, Novaro pitched her first feature film to the head of the film workers union. Novaro continues, "As soon as I entered his office, you know what the first words were that came out of his mouth? He tells me, 'What is driving you broads [viejas] to want to make movies?' I remember my face turning red, red, red, and thinking that I should respond, 'You clown, how dare you . . . say such stupidity?' But I didn't, I was too young then. Instead I said, 'I came to talk to you about a movie that I'm making, to negotiate with you, but I'm no longer interested. If you'll excuse me.'"[15]

That decision proved decisive. Novaro mostly works with cooperatives, cultivating a feminine aesthetic that, in her words, is "totally intentional—a focus that is rosy, soft, very ingenious, as though I were some kind of housewife making a movie."[16] Relying on subtle effects such as lighting and color, Novaro alters the cinematic practices of photographing women in Mexico and, with *Danzón*, reworks traditional forms of melodrama[17] so central to Mexican culture, helming "melodrama with another gender perspective," she interjects, "another cinematic taste . . . another sense of dialogue between women and men."[18]

Unlike the highly stylized theatrical tradition of studio filmmaking in Latin America, there is an authenticity to her characters, a true-to-life feel to stories in which it is women's actions that advance the plot. Novaro's penchant for blurring the boundaries between documentary and fiction dates to her early work with Cine Mujer: "Since the 1980s, I wanted to work with natural actors as well as professional actors, to go to real communities, and film in natural settings," she insists.[19]

In the early nineties, Novaro moved to Tijuana for ten months in order to absorb the texture of the borderlands and write *El jardín del Edén* (*The Garden of Eden*, 1994), on which she was collaborating with her sister Beatriz. This 1994 film probes the intersecting lives of three women who cross the border in search of a fresh start: Liz, a Chicana museum curator; Serena, a widowed mother of three; and Jane, an Anglo-American traveler.[20]

Previous Page: Director María Novaro displays her Marc'Aurelio Jury Award for Best Actress, presented to the entire female cast of *Las buenas hierbas* (*The Good Herbs*, 2010) at the 5th International Rome Film Festival. Right: Poster for *Danzón* (María Novaro, 1991).

Six years later, Novaro directed *Sin dejar huella* (*Without a Trace*, 2000), a road movie about two women, Ana (a Spanish art dealer) and Aurelia (a young mother of two) whose unrelated escape from police and narco-traffickers unite them on a journey across Mexico in search of freedom and a fresh start. "Of course I thought about *Thelma and Louise*, a movie that delights me," she confesses. "But I rebelled against the tragic destiny . . . and punishment they received for being daring women."[21] Novaro's take on a female road movie is wholly different. In *Sin dejar huella* bonding between women works to save, not punish or entrap characters.

El jardín del Edén and *Sin dejar huella* were co-productions made with French-Canadian and Spanish financing, an arrangement that guaranteed international distribution and exhibition but with a cost. As Novaro explains, "In my experience, a bigger budget is not synonymous with more creative freedom or greater control over my own movies, not at all."[22]

In her recent film, *Las buenas hierbas*, Novaro retained total creative control: "In contrast to the other two movies … I feel that for good or for bad, I did make the movie I desired."[23] Shot on digital video with her film students working as crew, Novaro drew from personal experience to make this heart-wrenching drama about a mother's deepening struggle with Alzheimer's and a daughter who bears witness to the painful unfolding of their lives. Long a staple of the genre of women's films, the mother-daughter bond in Novaro's film leads to a startling ending.[24]

Even as Novaro once noted that "she never set out to write a feminist manifesto,"[25] her films exude a tenacious feminist sensibility, one that enabled the emergence of a newer generation of filmmakers like Lucrecia Martel who reaped the benefits of "feminist influence and activism without necessarily identifying with its politics."[26]

LUCRECIA MARTEL

As a teenager, Lucrecia Martel obsessively videotaped a willing cast of sisters and brothers, teaching herself to use a brand new camcorder her father brought home by reading the manual front-to-back and replaying the video-recordings non-stop. Martel attributes her singular film grammar to these early experiments with the camera as well as to long siesta hours listening to her grandmother's supernatural stories:

"I appreciate my grandmother's terrifying stories because terror is something that denaturalizes reality . . . It seems to me that my pleasure for the world of horror, and of the fantastic has given me another relationship with reality . . . with a world . . . in which the rules are much more complex than those of the world of everyday life."[27]

On the aesthetic front, Lucrecia Martel is in a category by herself. Internationally recognized for her distinctive visual style, she designs sensually evocative films with disorienting shots, oblique angles, and audio tracks dense with mysterious off-screen sounds. Martel attributes her preference for off-center close-ups over establishing shots to her myopia.

Martel's international fame originated with *La ciénaga* (*The Swamp*, 2001), an award-winning film at many festivals, about a middle-class family vacationing in their dilapidated country estate during the dog days of summer. Set in the northwestern region of Argentina at the edge of the rainforest, *La ciénaga,* according to Martel,"proceeds through an accumulation of innocuous situations which often lead to nothing, but sometimes end fatally."[28] In its focus on the poetics of everyday life, the film's portrayal of family dynamics is neither sentimental nor overly dramatic, but one in which characters are possessed by an abundant sense of discomfort. Martel's films are all set in her birthplace, Salta, Argentina, where she grew up as the middle child of seven in a world similar to the one depicted in *La ciénaga*. In her Academy Visual History Interview, Martel notes: "Before the film was released, I showed it to my siblings and parents and one of my brothers said, 'This film will not be understood anywhere because it's as if you had attached a camera to us.'"

Initially studying animation in Avellaneda, Martel later attended the national film school in Buenos Aires, yet she roots her penchant for enigmatic stories fraught with ambiguity in the particularities of northwestern Argentina claiming, "In these societies, the supernatural permanently coexists with reality. It's not a magic realism but a continuity between the living and the dead, between the life of the living and the life of the dead within the living. A coexistence with divinity."[29]

Human coexistence with divinity is reflected in the miraculous apparition of the Virgin Mary on a water tank in *La ciénaga* and in *La niña santa's* (*The Holy Girl*, Lucrecia Martel, 2004) portrayal of the sexual musings of a fourteen-year-old Catholic schoolgirl obsessed with the redemption of a doctor who sexually molested her. For Martel, *The Holy Girl* "is a tale about good and evil, not a confrontation between good and evil, but about the difficulties of distinguishing one from the other."[30]

Ambiguity is the most honest place for a director when you deal with people's desires,"Martel insists.[31] The narrative universe in *La mujer sin cabeza* (*The Headless Woman*, Lucrecia Martel, 2008), her third feature film,is as ambiguous as it is disorienting and perplexing. The story deals with the psychological unraveling of a middle-aged dentist,

Vero, involved in an apparent hit-and-run. In a moment of distraction she hits an object while driving alone on a desolate highway, stops for a moment and then drives on, leaving audiences and Vero doubting whether she hit a dog or an indigenous boy. *La mujer sin cabeza* ends on an ambiguous note, without resolving its central dilemma.

Martel thwarts audience expectations for closure, leaving us with open-ended narratives that frequently test the boundaries of perception. "Usually someone thinks of cinema with a more linear narrative storyline," Martel declares. "But for me the point isn't to understand that one storyline, which is only one element among many . . . It has more to do with perception than understanding. So the movie is organized from a very subjective point of view."[32]

Tracing her storytelling techniques to the oral narrative tradition she inherited, Martel states, "My grandmother was very good at oral narration . . . [it] serves as my model . . . Oral narrative is more unraveled . . . it churns things around . . . All those elements one finds in a conversation: indirection, deviations, repetitions . . . the unintelligible is what I find interesting."[33]

Drawing from oral narrative, Martel develops audiovisual techniques that appeal to a fuller range of sensory experiences, like auditory perception. Whereas visual perception positions the viewer in

Left: Director Lucrecia Martel during production of *La mujer sin cabeza* (*The Headless Woman*, 2008).

Right: Still from *La niña santa* (*The Holy Girl*, Lucrecia Martel, 2004).

reality: "I think cinema gives directors, and in general people who work in films, the opportunity to use audiovisual narrative as a tool to break perception, and that is a political action."[36]

Martel's most ambitious project to date is the historical drama *Zama*, an adaptation of Argentinean novelist Antonio di Benedetto's 1956 novel of the same name. An international co-production, *Zama* portrays a disaffected eighteenth-century officer of the Spanish Crown whose monotonous life takes an unexpected turn. According to Martel, *Zama* "is also that moment in which a man prepares himself to live more fully. And when the opportunity arises and means risking his life, he is willing to go."[37] Martel's fourth feature is filmed in the geographic region of El Gran Chaco Gualamba, (located in Paraguay, Bolivia, and Argentina) and is scheduled for release in 2017.

PATRICIA CARDOSO

In 2002, Colombian-born director Patricia Cardoso directed *Real Women Have Curves*, the first Latina feature film to receive multiple awards at the Sundance Film Festival. An adaptation of Josefina López's play,[38] Cardoso's box-office hit tells the compelling story of a generational conflict between a Chicana daughter and mother. Set in an East L.A. garment sweatshop, this coming-of-age drama stars America Ferrera as Ana, a college-bound recipient of a scholarship to Columbia University and Lupe Ontiveros as Carmen, an overbearing mother determined to keep her daughter working in the factory. A film with remarkable hints of soulfulness, *Real Women Have Curves* won both the Audience Award and the Special Jury Prize at Sundance. "I didn't get along with my mother for many years," Cardoso confesses in her Academy Visual History Interview. "That's why *Real Women Have Curves* is,

a hierarchical relation over what she observes, in the world of sound, as Martel interjects, "the hierarchies are less clear . . . one is immersed in a world that is much more ambiguous, less referential."[34] The non-hierarchical orientation of Martel's cosmology also reflects her political perspective about racial and class hierarchies in northwestern Argentina.

In subtle but piercing ways, her films frequently touch upon the dynamics between the region's white elite and the largely indigenous workers, as in *Nueva Argirópolis* (*New Argirópolis*, Lucrecia Martel, 2010), a short film made for Argentina's bicentenary

celebration. Here, Martel features a chorus of voices speaking the indigenous languages of the Salta province, capturing her deep appreciation for the rich cultural diversity often negated in Argentina. "It's incredible that this vast richness is not promoted by the tourist industry . . . As if we're negating it— something very brutal and awkward. Devaluating the worlds that remain disempowered is a form of maintaining them there."[35]

The immersion in a fuller range of sensory experiences also reflects Martel's philosophical view about the role perception plays in transforming

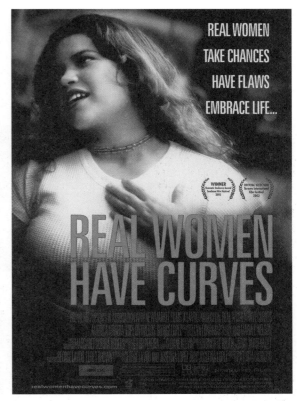

for me, about that relationship between a mother and a daughter who love each other, but get along horribly . . . It's a love story between a mother and a daughter but the daughter has to go far away. I went 5,000 miles away!"[39]

Cardoso grew up in Bogotá, the daughter of the first female architect to win Colombia's National Architecture Award and a father who inspired her love for nature and pre-Columbian art. After graduating from the Universidad de los Andes, Bogotá, with a degree from the Department of Anthropology (including coursework in archeology), Cardoso worked on excavations near indigenous and Afro-Colombian communities where she first heard oral histories recited by indigenous children.

For graduate school, she opted to channel her love for storytelling into filmmaking, as she explained in her interview for the Fulbright Fellowship to UCLA: "I want to study cinema to tell those incredible histories that I heard from indigenous children and Afro-Colombian cultures."[40] Her first student film at UCLA, *Cartas al niño Dios* (*Letters to Child God*,

Left: Producer Lita Stantic, Alejandro Urdapilleta, Maria Alche, director Lucrecia Martel, Mercedes Morán, and Mia Maestro at the Cannes Film Festival for *La niña santa* (*The Holy Girl*) in 2004.

Center Right: America Ferrera and Lupe Ontiveros at the Toronto Film Festival in 2002. Far Right: Poster for *Real Women Have Curves* (Patricia Cardoso, 2002).

Patricia Cardoso, 1991), was exhibited in fifty international festivals and won over twenty awards totaling $50,000. *The Water Carrier of Cucunuba* (1996), a short film based on a true story about her grandfather—who in 1926 performed one of the first cataract operations in Colombia—won the Academy of Motion Picture Arts and Science's Gold Medal for Best Student Film.

Prior to *Real Women Have Curves*, Cardoso worked as programmer of Latin American films at Sundance. Recipient of the first Ida Lupino Student Award for Best Female Director presented by the Directors Guild of America, Cardoso has directed a number of short films and made-for-TV movies, including a Hallmark film starring Sonia Braga and

a Lifetime film with Lupe Ontiveros as a Latina doctor. "I had a hard time casting Lupe as a medical professional because they [Lifetime executives] said the character was a man and I had changed it to a woman. Then they said, 'But there are no Latina doctors.' I replied, 'That's precisely the point, she is an extraordinary character.' It was a great struggle but in the end, they allowed me to cast her. And Lupe later told me that it was the first time she'd ever played a doctor . . . during her entire career, she has always played domestic workers."[41]

Despite this impressive record of accomplishments, Cardoso finds the film studios virtually impenetrable for a Latina. On seven occasions Cardoso has been one of two finalists for director of big-budget (over $30 million) studio films, yet she's never been selected. "The way it works in Hollywood," as she explains, "first you are interviewed by one of the producers and if selected, you are then interviewed by the studio executive . . . the two finalists are then interviewed by the studio president. In all seven projects, I was one of two finalists interviewed by studio presidents but they did not choose me but rather the other person. Coincidentally all were Anglo-Saxon white males."[42]

Notwithstanding these setbacks, Cardoso advises the future generation of filmmakers to maintain a stalwart mindset: "It's not the strongest that survives, it's the one who adapts to the rapid changes . . . One needs great perseverance and resistance to rejection because for every 'Yes,' there will be fifty 'Nos,' so it's very difficult to move forward. In this sense, teaching has helped me a great deal to maintain my mental health because . . . one feels deflated and can't keep going, so one has to have resistance and find a way to manage that."[43]

LOURDES PORTILLO

Lourdes Portillo is a versatile filmmaker with a poet's eye for detail. Her unorthodox approach to filmmaking pushes against widely held documentary norms, blending realist with poetic techniques, stretching the parameters of nonfiction through the use of humor, satire and allegory, as she ventures into the larger social and political dynamics of Latina/o communities. For years, Portillo has consistently aligned her work with social justice concerns, as she affirms in a recent Academy Visual History Interview: "I think basically at the center is an artist that is concerned about Chicanos, about human rights, about women, children, and men too . . . I went to Catholic school," she adds, "And you know Catholic school really does teach you some compassion."[44]

Portillo's concern with issues of social justice was shaped by her earliest childhood memories. Born in Chihuahua, Mexico, she migrated as a child with her family to Los Angeles, California. "It was so painful," she confesses. "We moved from a place where you . . . and your culture is cherished . . . to a place where you feel that somebody wants to destroy you . . . and you are not wanted."[45] Along with her father's gift of a camera, this experience cultivated an interest in image making: "I always had a hobby of photography . . . and when I was going to grammar school, I won a contest in photography."

As an adult in Los Angeles, Portillo worked with friend Sally Loeb on a documentary for Britannica Films. She later married, moved to San Francisco, and enrolled in the San Francisco Art Institute—a decision that proved decisive in cementing her life-long passion for the art of filmmaking. "My interest in cinema," as she discloses, "originated with poetry, with experimental film, and with experimenting with art."[46] Before enrolling in the Art Institute, she had made films during the early seventies as a member of the Marxist collective, Cine Manifest.[47] Her first film, *Después del terremoto* (*After the Earthquake*, Lourdes Portillo and Nina Serrano, 1979) is a narrative short co-directed with Nina Serrano in 1979, portraying gender conflicts in the life of a Nicaraguan migrant in San Francisco who fled during the Somoza regime.[48]

Portillo established her reputation as a documentary filmmaker with the Oscar-nominated *Las Madres: The Mothers of the Plaza de Mayo* (Lourdes Portillo and Susana Muñoz, 1986), co-directed with Argentinean-born Susana Muñoz. During the final years of the military dictatorship in Argentina, Portillo and Muñoz started working on *Las Madres* and later recorded interviews during the first hundred days of the country's return to democracy. The documentary narrates state-sponsored terrorism against civilians, waged by a military regime that ruled Argentina from 1976–1983 and disappeared around 30,000 dissidents. *Las Madres* focuses on the courageous struggle of mothers who defied the dictatorship by staging banned demonstrations in the most guarded public plaza of Argentina, the Plaza de Mayo, unequivocally disregarding the military junta's authority.

In highlighting the mothers' voices and the process of 'radicalization,' rather than victimization, *Las Madres* proves inspirational for viewers around the world because it exemplifies how middle-aged women cultivated a collective politics and channeled their own personal pain as mothers into radical action. As Portillo adds, "The thing about *The Mothers of the Plaza de Mayo* which I've never encountered since that time is that they were so valiant . . . never afraid . . . they were a big, big influence on me . . . they were like warrior geniuses."[49]

Portillo's first subjective documentary is *The Devil Never Sleeps* (1984)—a "melodocumystery," a term coined by Portillo to describe its hybrid style. The documentary probes the unresolved death of her favorite uncle, Oscar, who died under mysterious circumstances in Mexico. In the course of her investigation, Portillo pierces through the veneer of family secrets, conflicting testimonies, and surprising contradictions in the personal and political life of her beloved uncle. *The Devil Never Sleeps* captures the disconcerting schism of her vision: Portillo's adoration of Tío Oscar and her, at times, vexed position in the family. For audiences familiar with Mexican political culture, the allegorical element of the documentary is palpable: the intrigues, deception, and hypocrisy of this private family (Portillo's) personify the corrupt politics of the public, national family of the PRI, the political party that—until the election of Vicente Fox in 2000—had ruled Mexico for over seventy years. Starring as niece-detective-documentarian, Portillo narrates the story in a hybrid style, blending documentary with telenovela aesthetics, gossip with home movies and legends, simultaneously foregrounding complex issues about *la familia* for Chicanas/os and Mexicans on both sides of the border.

Although Portillo's parents appreciated the critical, postmodernist approach to documenting Tío Oscar's story, the film severed relations with her extended family. "Well, what wasn't expected was that my uncles and aunts were so angry with me when I finished the film . . . it was like another telenovela. My aunt died a year afterwards and my cousin said,'You killed her . . . because she saw that film and it damned near killed her.'"[50]

Left: Director Patricia Cardoso and other winners of the 23rd Student Academy Awards, 1996.

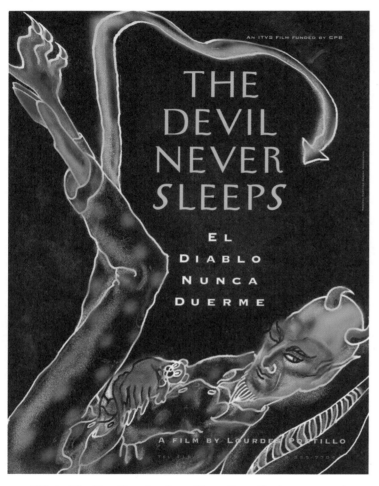

THE DEVIL NEVER SLEEPS

EL DIABLO NUNCA DUERME

A FILM BY LOURDES PORTILLO

of the Dead, 1988) also co-directed with Muñoz, the filmmakers juxtapose lyrical with didactic narrations of the Day of the Dead celebration among indigenous and Mexican communities in Oaxaca, Mexico and its revival in San Francisco, California, during the 1970s when the Chicana/o cultural arts movement, under the direction of Ralph Maradiaga, began organizing exhibitions and an annual parade in the Mission district.

Portillo's tribute to the Tejana singer Selena's legacy, *Corpus: A Home Movie for Selena* (Lourdes Portillo, 1999), is woven through stories of fandom, patriarchy, gender, and queer performances. Her most recent film, *Al más allá* (Lourdes Portillo, 2008), pushes even further against standard documentary norms. Blending documentary with story-bound techniques, *Al más allá* features Mexican actress Ofelia Medina playing the part of Portillo, along with a fictional crew, as the documentarian Portillo investigates the impact of the global drug trafficking industry on the lives of three fishermen from a small fishing community on Mexico's Mayan Riviera.

Among her finest documentaries to date is *Señorita extraviada* (*Missing Young Woman*, 2001), a compelling investigation of the phenomenon of feminicide in the border city of Ciudad Juárez, Chihuahua. At the time of its release in 2001, close to 300 women and girls had been murdered and hundreds more disappeared; many were held in captivity and subjected to extreme forms of sexual violence, rape, and torture. The film documents the campaign for social justice headed primarily by mothers of the disappeared and murdered victims and supported by local women's rights activists.

In documenting the psychic trauma that family members live and continually re-live with each new report of a murder or disappearance, Portillo confronted an enormous problem of representation. How does one represent the dead in a way that does not further desecrate their bodies or re-traumatize their families, but is respectful of their grief and honors the memories of the women and girls who were murdered? That dilemma was solved during the editing process with editor Vivian Hillgrove who said to Portillo, "I feel like those 200 girls are behind us, and they're editing with us, and they're guiding us. So let's just follow them. Yes, the girls are with us and we have to represent them right."[51] Working with Hillgrove, Portillo drew from the local justice campaign's use of religious symbolism. To their credit, not a single dead body appears in the film, nonetheless the haunting presence of the victims is summoned literally, through the placement of photographs, and figuratively with depictions of crosses and soundtrack as a Requiem for the dead.

By portraying feminicide on the borderlands, Portillo aimed to change the hearts and minds of its viewers. "The whole intention of the film was to create a kind of consciousness," she says, "to incite people to act, and it did that."[52] Portillo became a crusader for women's rights and the campaign to end gender violence, screening the film before international audiences and raising awareness about the persistence of impunity throughout the region. Winning over twenty international awards, including Amnesty International's first Award for an Artist and

With *The Devil* and other films, Portillo has waged a gentle revolution in documentary aesthetics. In the wake of the Quincentenary, Portillo collaborated with the comedy trio Culture Clash to produce the experimental satirical video, *Columbus on Trial* (Lourdes Portillo, 1992), as part of the hemispheric counter-commemorations of Christopher Columbus' fateful voyage. In *La ofrenda* (*The Days*

film can be used in the service of the unprotected and documentary can take a stance, and inform, activate, promote understanding and compassion . . . create a kind of consciousness to incite people to act."[54]

Ruminating about her life's work, Portillo says, "I'm just really happy that I've made the films that I've made, because they illuminate the life of people such as myself. I've made subjective films and I have followed my instincts because it's part of the historical presence of Mexican people, Latino people, people of color in this country . . . I hope that young filmmakers do the same thing because we have to see ourselves in film, we have to see ourselves in documentary, we have to see ourselves everywhere the way we are."[55] Like Patricia Cardoso and María Novaro, Portillo is dedicated to mentoring a younger generation of filmmakers who will continue the legacy of creating films for social change.

the Néstor Almendros award from Human Rights Watch, *Señorita extraviada* has screened before members of state and intergovernmental bodies like the European Parliament, the U.S. Congress, and the International Criminal Court, and forums like the 9th World Summit of Nobel Peace Laureates in Paris. Apart from its screening at film festivals and intergovernmental human rights venues, the documentary was shown before organizing and activist audiences in Latin America, the U.S., and Europe.

In the span of four decades, Portillo has consistently embraced an aesthetic of social justice rooted in Latin America's *Tercer Cine*. Its common denominator, as one of Third Cinema's exponents Argentinean filmmaker Fernando Birri declares, is a "poetics of transformation . . . a creative energy which, through cinema, aims to modify the reality upon which it is projected."[53] The poetics and politics of Portillo's films share this passion for changing the social worlds. According to Portillo, "The art of

Left: Poster for *The Devil Never Sleeps* (Lourdes Portillo, 1994).

Right: Director Lourdes Portillo interviewing a subject during the filming of *Missing Young Woman* (2001).

WOMEN IN OTHER BEHIND-THE-SCENES ROLES

Making films from a gender perspective is not the only way women have contributed to cinema. Long relegated to obscurity, women working in key creative behind-the-scenes roles—and not just *on* screen—have made major contributions to the film industry, working above the line as producers, cinematographers, and writers, as well as below the line as production assistants and editors.

In the United States, Latina silent film star Beatriz Michelena was also executive producer and co-owner of the California Motion Picture Corporation in San Francisco.[56] Directors Mimí Derba, co-founder of Azteca Film Productions, and María Cantoni made significant inroads into silent cinema of Mexico,[57] as did Gabriela von Bussenius Vega in Chile, and María V. de Celestini and Emilia Saleni in Argentina.[58] Despite their century-long presence, behind-the-scenes, women continue to be grossly underrepresented in every national film industry.

Studies on the employment of women and Latinos in the Hollywood industry reveal blatant

gender and racial inequities. These injustices have become a heated topic in recent years. According to "The Celluloid Ceiling," an annual report that tracks women's employment in the industry, women

directors represented a mere nineteen percent of the top grossing 250 films in 2015, a figure on par with the percentage in 2001.[59] In her Academy Visual History Interview, Patricia Cardoso added that "women of color represent less than two percent."[60]

In Latin America, female producers and writers like Bertha Navarro and Paz Alicia Garcíadiego, both of whom were interviewed as part of the Academy's *Pacific Standard Time: LA/LA* project, and Lita Stantic,[61] have undoubtedly diversified the gender demographics of the film industry in their respective home countries and contributed a distinct cultural sensibility to Hollywood's global hegemony. However, the difference between working in the industry as a woman and making a film from a female perspective is highlighted by screenwriter Garcíadiego, who considers her screenplays to be "the diametric opposite of films made by Hollywood," even as she rejects gender or racial identification: "I categorically refuse to be considered a minority, a woman, a Latina, that word is offensive to me, like a dwarf. I don't like being a minority so there's no room for me. I don't have exemplary stories to tell."[62] Like her partner Arturo Ripstein who refused

to be identified as a Latin American filmmaker by the Sundance Film Institute, Garcíadiego situates her work in universal (world cinema) rather than particular (national cinema) terms.[63]

Bertha Navarro has worked as a producer for over four decades. Her career began at an auspicious moment in Mexican history, a time when a left-leaning generation regarded film as a vehicle for changing the social order. Initially working on documentaries about the student protest movements, the Tlatelolco massacre, and mass mobilizations during the 1968 Olympics in Mexico City, she landed her first job as producer for Paul Leduc's *Reed, México insurgente* (*Reed: Insurgent Mexico*, 1970), a film that ushered in a

Far Left: Beatriz Michelena in *Salomy Jane* (William Nigh, 1914). Center Right: Producer Bertha Navarro displaying her awards at her home in Mexico City, 2016. Far Right: Director María Novaro with Robert Redford, undated.

refreshing style of filmmaking in Mexico. In contrast to the "official" Mexican industry's proclivity for comedies made with "super large cameras," as Navarro explains in her recent Academy Visual History Interview with Lourdes Portillo. "With *Reed . . .* we used hand-held cameras, direct sound, things that weren't done at the time . . . It was filmed as if it were a documentary and it was done in sepia, which was like the films of 1910. So we made a film as if we were making a documentary in the Mexican Revolution."[64]

Since then Navarro has produced dozens of internationally-acclaimed films including director Guillermo del Toro's *El laberinto del fauno* (*Pan's Labyrinth,* 2006); John Sayles's *Men with Guns* (1997); and *Cabeza de Vaca* (1991) by Nicolás Echeverría. Earlier in her career, she was also line-producer for Gregory Nava's *El Norte* (1983).[65]

Latin American women have also made their mark as screenwriters for major motion pictures. In 1985, Paz Alicia Garcíadiego started her thirty-year collaboration with one of Mexico's most prolific directors, Arturo Ripstein, first adapting Juan Rulfo's *El gallo de oro* into a screenplay for *El imperio de la fortuna* (*The Empire of Fortune*, 1986). An avid reader who grew up listening to her grandmother's stories, as did Martel, Garcíadiego has penned over a dozen densely complex screenplays that probe the wicked side of human nature including art house favorites *Principio y fin* (*The Beginning and the End*, 1993), *La reina de la noche* (*The Queen of the Night,* 1994), *Profundo carmesí* (*Deep Crimson*, 1996), and *La perdición de los hombres* (*The Ruination of Men*, 2000). Garcíadiego's proclivity for dark comedy and melodrama have markedly shaped the "world of Arturo Ripstein's films," described by one critic as "a sordid place of tormented souls, shifting morality, violent acts, absurdity, and wretchedness."[66]

Not only have female producers and writers like Bertha Navarro and Paz Alicia Garcíadiego diversified the film industry, but they often contribute a distinct cultural sensibility which counters the hegemonic discourse that Lucrecia Martel maintains "is very pre-formed by Hollywood because the model for narrative commercial cinema has permeated the world in such an insoluble manner."[67] As Bertha Navarro adds: "In Mexico . . . there is a very great totalitarianism in terms of our film exhibition, specifically the big Hollywood films control ninety-five percent of the projection screens in our country . . . I believe that the world's voices are important. And in order for future generations to learn about other cultures and other places, cinema is truly important, because . . . it's the historical legacy of other cultures, because the diversity of the world is just as important. Even though we are all human and share similar things, there are other ways of understanding and of living these things. For example, my viewing an Iranian film opens up the world; suddenly I can look into that place. And I believe that this is the great legacy of cinematography, that one can look into and see other histories, other stories, other cultures, and hear other languages, see different faces."[68]

The diversity of women's stories, histories, cultures, and languages is reflected in the films made by the women filmmakers profiled in this essay. With their women-centered stories, directors like Patricia Cardoso, María Novaro, Lucrecia Martel, and Lourdes Portillo have left an enduring imprint on audiences, national, and world film cultures. As the documentation of films helmed by women continues to expand, so too will our appreciation for the significance of the transformative force of different female perspectives in shaping a cinema of her own.

DR. ROSA-LINDA FREGOSO

Professor and Former Chair of Latin American and Latino Studies, University of California, Santa Cruz

Dr. Fregoso has written extensively on issues of human rights, feminicide, intersectional violence, cinema and culture in the Américas. Her major publications include: *Terrorizing Women: Feminicide in the Américas*, co-edited with Cynthia Bejarano, Duke University Press, 2010); *Feminicidio en América Latina*, (2011); and *meXicana Encounters: The Making of Social Identities on the Borderlands* (2003), winner of the MLA's Prize, U.S./Latino/a, Chicano/a Literary and Cultural Studies. Her *The Bronze Screen: Chicana and Chicano Film Culture* (1993), is the first single-authored book on Chicana/o film and culture. She also edited *The Devil Never Sleeps and Other Films by Lourdes Portillo* (2001); and *Miradas de Mujer*, co-edited with Norma Iglesias (1998). Fregoso holds a Ph.D. from the Language, Society and Culture Program (Literature and Communication) at the University of California, San Diego.

Left: Poster for *Pan's Labyrinth* (Guillermo del Toro, 2006).

Right: Alicia Paz Garcíadiego and Arturo Ripstein at the Venice Film Festival for *La calle de la amargura* (*Bleak Street*) in 2015.

NOTES

1. I borrow this concept "a cinema of her own" from Patricia White's insightful book *Women's Cinema, World Cinema* (Durham and London: Duke University Press, 2015).

2. Academy Visual History with María Novaro, interviewed by Lourdes Portillo in Mexico City, September 25, 2015.

3. Of these, 35% helmed documentaries and 19% women directors worked on narrative features. See: Martha M. Lauzen, "Women in Independent Films, 2015–16," *Center for the Study of Women in Television and Film* (May 2016). (PDF available at: http://womenintvfilm.sdsu.edu/files/2016%20Independent_Women_Report.pdf

4. Quoted in White, *Women's Cinema, World Cinema*, 12.

5. One such example of "a cinema of her own" from an intersectional perspective is writer-director Aurora Guerrero, who made the first feature film by a Chicana to screen at the Sundance Film Festival. Set in Huntington Park, a largely Mexican neighborhood of Los Angeles, *Mosquita y Mari's* (Aurora Guerrero, 2012) lesbian subtext showcases two high school classmates from immigrant families, who surprisingly experience mutual sexual attraction.

6. Academy Visual History with María Novaro, interviewed by Lourdes Portillo in Mexico City, September 25, 2015. In an earlier interview, Novaro stated: "I like it very much when people come away thinking 'Only a woman could have made that film." Quoted in Tim Golden, "'Danzón Glides to a Soft Mexican Rhythm,'"review of *Danzón*, directed by María Novaro, *The New York Times*, (October 11, 1992).

7. Academy Visual History with María Novaro, interviewed by Lourdes Portillo in Mexico City, September 25, 2015.

8. From María Novaro, Director's Statement for *Danzón* (1991) where she writes: "I'm always asking myself questions about what it is to be a woman. Do we see the world in a different way? I often think about my grandmother, my aunts, my daughters, my friends, and myself. The women that I know. To invent stories and to play with the possibilities of their lives is something which enthuses me immensely. It is, surely, a way of exploring the feminine soul."

9. The Ariel is the Mexican equivalent of an Oscar.

10. The film won Ariel awards for Best First Work, Best Screenplay, Best Supporting Female Actor, and Best Supporting Male Actor; and awards at the Havana Film Festival and the Latino Film Festival in New York.

11. Academy Visual History with María Novaro, interviewed by Lourdes Portillo in Mexico City, September 25, 2015.

12. Acronym for Centro Universitario de Estudios Cinematográficos.

13. Academy Visual History with María Novaro, interviewed by Lourdes Portillo in Mexico City, September 25, 2015.

14. As Novaro expands, "the union would not allow me to hire Marie-Christine Camus to film my movies because she was a woman." Ibid.

15. Ibid.

16. Golden, "'Danzón' Glides to a Soft Mexican Rhythm."

17. Traditional Mexican melodramas represent an idealized vision of Mexico, Mexican motherhood as an embodiment of the nation, and women in terms of the binary "virgin/mother-whore."

18. Academy Visual History with María Novaro, interviewed by Lourdes Portillo in Mexico City, September 25, 2015.

19. Ibid.

20. With the film's utterly frank appraisal of the vitality and desperation of border life, Novaro aimed to spark a bi-national dialogue: "I feel that I narrated with much sincerity the turbulence of encounter and dis-encounter . . . of those on the border. And I did so thinking more about Mexicans who don't really know how to see the border, because that's who I am." Ibid.

21. Ibid.

22. *Lola* and *Danzón* were both financed by Television Española, but Novaro retained creative control. For *El jardín del Edén*, she was forced to hire Canadian actors to play U.S. characters, and strongly pressured to cut the film by twenty minutes. *Sin dejar huella* was originally written for two Mexican female characters from different class backgrounds yet ended up with Spanish actor Aitana Sánchez-Gijón in the lead. Her salary was exorbitant—"equivalent to the salaries of all the Mexicans," Novaro discloses, "including mine and other actors . . . she earned the same as the entire Mexican group." Ibid.

23. Academy Visual History with María Novaro, interviewed by Lourdes Portillo in Mexico City, September 25, 2015.

24. As she intimates in the interview with Portillo: "I wanted to relay that one's life is a cycle that ends . . . [but] that it also remains there in nature, that nature continues and that we are a small part of nature." Ibid.

25. Quoted in Golden, "'Danzón' Glides to a Soft Mexican Rhythm."

26. White, *Women's Cinema, World Cinema*, 18.

27. Academy Visual History with Lucretia Martel, interviewed by Lourdes Portillo in Hollywood, October 3, 2014.

28. Lucrecia Martel, Director's Statement for *La ciénaga* (2001).

29. Academy Visual History with Lucrecia Martel, interviewed by Lourdes Portillo in Hollywood, October 3, 2014. In an earlier interview, Martel rejected the label of magic realism as "fascist," to describe her work. (See B. Ruby Rich, "Making Argentina Matter Again," *New York Times*, September 30, 2001).

30. Director's Statement for *The Holy Girl* (2004).

31. Academy Visual History with Lucrecia Martel, interviewed by Lourdes Portillo in Hollywood, October 3, 2014.

32. Mark Olsen, "Questions, But No Easy Answers," *Los Angeles Times*, August 9, 2009.

33. Academy Visual History with Lucrecia Martel, interviewed by Lourdes Portillo in Hollywood, October 3, 2014.

34. Ibid.

35. Ibid.

36. Ibid

37. Quoted in John Hopewell, "Much Awaited Production, One

of Latin America's Biggest, Begins Shooting," *Variety*, May 20, 2015. http://variety.com/2015/film/global/cannes-lucrecia-martel-rolls-on-zama-exclusive-1201501683/

38. The play was adapted into a screenplay by López and George LaVoo.

39. Academy Visual History with Patricia Cardoso, interviewed by Lourdes Portillo in Hollywood, April 14, 2015.

40. Ibid.

41. Ibid.

42. Ibid.

43. Ibid.

44. Academy Visual History with Lourdes Portillo, interviewed by Sienna McLean-LoGreco in Hollywood, December 5, 2013.

45. Ibid.

46. Ibid.

47. In Cine Manifest she first worked as Stephen Lighthill's assistant in the collective feature, *Over, Under, Sideways, Down* (Eugene Corr, Peter Gessner and Steve Wax, 1977). See Rosa-Linda Fregoso, "Introduction," in *Lourdes Portillo: The Devil Never Sleeps and Other Films*, ed. Rosa-Linda Fregoso (Austin: University of Texas Press, 2001), 1–23.

48. For an extensive analysis of these and other films by Portillo, see ibid.

49. Academy Visual History with Lourdes Portillo, interviewed by Sienna McLean-LoGreco in Hollywood, December 5, 2013.

50. Ibid.

51. Ibid.

52. Lourdes Portillo, "Filming *Señorita Extraviada*," *Aztlán* 28:2 (2003): 233.

53. Fernando Birri, "For a Nationalist, Realist, Critical and Popular Cinema," in *New Latin American Cinema*, vol. 1: *Theory,*

Practices, and Transnational Articulations, ed. M.T. Martin (Detroit: Wayne State University Press, 1997), 96.

54. Lourdes Portillo, "Filming *Señorita Extraviada*," 229.

55. Academy Visual History with Lourdes Portillo, interviewed by Sienna McLean-LoGreco in Hollywood, December 5, 2013.

56. See Rosa-Linda Fregoso, *meXicana Encounters: The Making of Social Identities on the Borderlands* (Berkeley: University of California Press, 2003).

57. Concha Irazábal Martín, *La otra América*, (Madrid: horas y HORAS editorial, 2001).

58. Joanna Hershfield and Patricia Torres San Martín, "Writing the History of Latin American Women Working in the Silent Film Industry," in *Women Film Pioneers Project, Center for Digital Research and Scholarship*, eds. Jane Gaines, Radha Vatsal, and Monica Dall' Asta (New York, NY: Columbia University Libraries, 2013), https://wfpp.cdrs.columbia.edu/essay/writing-the-history-of-latin-american-women-working-in-the-silent-film-industry/ last consulted May 5, 2016. In Argentina, Emilia Saleni directed *La niña del bosque (The Girl from the Woods*, 1916) and *El pañuelo de Clarita (Clarita's Handkerchief*, 1917), while María V. de Celestini directed her sole feature film, *Mi derecho (My Right*, 1920) in 1920 (see Irazábal Martín).

59. See: Martha M. Lauzen, "The Celluloid Ceiling: Behind the Scenes Employment of Women on the Top 250 Films in 2015," *Center for the Study of Women in Television and Film* (2016), available at: http://womenintvfilm.sdsu.edu/research/. *The Latino Media Gap* study charts a similar disparity for Latinos and Latinas in mainstream media. Seventeen percent of the U.S. population, Latino and Latin Americans in Hollywood represent 2.3% of directors; 2.2% producers; and 6% writers for the years 2010–13. Of these, the overwhelming majority were men. See Frances Negrón-Muntaner with Chelsea Abbas, Luis Figueroa, and Samuel Robson, "The Latino Media Gap: A Report on the State of Latinos in U.S. Media," *NALIP and The Center for the Study of Race and Ethnicity, National Foundation for the Arts* (2014). Available at: http://www.cser.columbia.edu/#!links-1/tssmd.

60. Academy Visual History with Patricia Cardoso, interviewed by Lourdes Portillo in Hollywood, April 14, 2015.

61. Since 1972, Lita Stantic has been one of the most dynamic promoters of Argentinean cinema, creating the production and distribution company, GEA Cinematográfica, and launching highly celebrated independent filmmakers like María Luisa Bembergand Lucrecia Martel. B. Ruby Rich calls Stantic the "godmother of the New Argentine generation." She has produced more than twenty features, over half by women, including María Luisa Bemberg's *Momentos (Moments*, 1981), *Señora de nadie (Nobody's Woman*, 1982), *Miss Mary* (1986), *Yo la peor de todas (Me, the Worst of All*, 1990), *De eso no se habla (We Don't Speak About That*, 1993), and Martel's Salta trilogy: *La ciénaga, La niña santa, and La mujer sin cabeza*. In 1988 Stantic collaborated with a group of Argentinean artists to organize the Mar de Plata Festival of Women and Cinema and two years later she directed *Un muro de silencio (A Wall of Silence*, 1990; 1993 release), a film reflecting on the traumatic effects of military repression in Argentina. See Catherine Grant, "The Cultural Salience of an Argentine Female Producer," available at: https://www.scribd.com/document/287872297/catherine-grant-on-lita-stanticand B. Ruby Rich, "Making Argentina Matter Again," *New York Times*, September 30, 2001.

62. Academy Visual History with Paz Alicia Garcíadiego, interviewed by Lourdes Portillo in Mexico City, September 23, 2015.

63. See Academy Visual History with Paz Alicia Garcíadiego, interviewed by Lourdes Portillo in Mexico City, September 23, 2015.

64. Academy Visual History with Bertha Navarro, interviewed by Lourdes Portillo in Mexico City, September 26, 2015. Later, Navarro directed *Nicaragua, los que harán la libertad (Nicaragua, Those Who'll Make Freedom*, 1978), a documentary about the Sandinista's struggle against the Somoza regime that won the Critics Award at the Cannes Film Festival.

65. Also produced del Toro's *Cronos* (Guillermo del Toro, 1993), and *El espinazo del diablo (The Devil's Backbone*, Guillermo del Toro, 2001).

66. Quoted in David Rooney, "The Ruination of Men," review of *The Ruination of Men*, directed by Arturo Ripstein, *Variety* (October 3, 2000).

67. Academy Visual History with Lucrecia Martel, interviewed by Lourdes Portillo in Hollywood, October 3, 2014.

REVERSE ANGLE/
CONTRACAMPO
LATIN AMERICAN
FILMMAKERS
ENVISION HOLLYWOOD

BY: CATHERINE L. BENAMOU

To the memory of
Héctor Babenco and María Elena Velasco

The prevailing view within academic and critical discourse has been that Latin American and Latinx[1] cinemas have developed largely despite, or in direct opposition to, the pervasive influence of the Hollywood film industry. This perspective is hardly surprising, given the dampening effect on national cinemas of (1) early ownership of major movie theaters by Hollywood studios in Latin American metropoles, (2) the heavy taxation on the exhibition of Mexican-produced cinema in the U.S. in the 1950s, (3) the MPAA's historically powerful opposition to Latin American protective quota systems since World War II,[2] not to mention, (4) the seductive appeal of the Hollywood star system and game-defining audiovisual technology displayed in productions and experienced in well-equipped movie theaters and other exhibition platforms. In vigorous response to these intrusions, several governments, beginning in the 1940s, created film finance mechanisms (such as the Banco Cinematográfico in Mexico), and have introduced protective measures to safeguard distribution channels and screen space for national productions.

Meanwhile, in the midst of new cinematic waves across the globe from the late 1950s to 1970s, Latin American film theorists emphasized the need to break with the industrial model of production and character-centered narratives associated with Hollywood genre filmmaking.[3] These exhortations were echoed in film practice with a push towards a realist "laying bare" of socio-environmental reality and a modernist experimental impulse, represented in various alternate formats by Latin American filmmakers.[4] In one way *and* another, the tone was set for the internationally recognized stream of Latin American art cinema that followed: an adherence to socially and politically relevant themes and storylines, a decentering of conventional heroic figures in favor of marginal characters, a cultivation, rather than a sidestepping of artisanal production methods, an insistence on the inscription of place, an embrace of social friction, and cultural suppleness, even at the risk of losing the Hollywood-habituated Latin American spectator. Films such as Alfonso Cuarón's *Y tu mamá también* (2002), Tata Amaral's *Antônia* (2006), and Lucrecia Martel's *La ciénaga* (*The Swamp,* 2001) come to mind.

Paralleling and at times, intersecting with these trends is nearly a century of creative engagement by Latin American and Latinx filmmakers, screenwriters, and cinematographers with Hollywood as both a producing-distributing apparatus and a powerful purveyor of aesthetic and cultural paradigms. My task in this essay is to locate these points of intersection and to adopt a reverse angle through which the protean forms taken by these representations, the surrounding popular film culture, and the larger city of Los Angeles that has given them life, can be studied. The North-South contact zone[5] that comes into view is more nuanced and spectral than starkly adversarial, pointing to a level of interaction and exchange intensified in the wake of recent transborder co-productions and collaborations. What emerges is a palimpsest of portrayals that complicates, rather than displaces, the still-relevant concepts of national and artistically independent cinema. Even the most

irreverent, iconoclastic references to Hollywood in films of the late 1960s, such as *Memorias del subdesarrollo* (*Memories of Underdevelopment*, Tomás Gutiérrez Alea, 1968) and *O bandido da luz vermelha* (*The Red Light Bandit,* Rogério Sganzerla, 1968) beg a reframing of this history of interaction. The method of the reframing will elucidate the ambivalence and fascination, the processes of transculturation and acts of counter-appropriation as well as of contestation and deviation, which have taken root in the furrows of this zone.

Although the history of this engagement can be traced over most of the twentieth century, reaching its apex in the years during and following World War II, I focus mainly on the period from the eighties to the new millennium, when the possibility for Latin American directors and cinematographers to actually work in Hollywood opened up once again,[6] and a growing diasporic Latinx audience north of the Rio Grande attracted the attention of producers and distributors throughout the Americas. In an era when Spanish-language films from the Mexican Golden Age were still being screened at repertory movie theaters in downtown Los Angeles, San Francisco, Central and Southwestern Texas, Chicago, Miami, Jersey City, and uptown Manhattan,[7] Hollywood launched a "Hispanic Decade" that welcomed first features by a new generation of Latinx filmmakers.[8] The decade also enhanced the possibility of durable careers for Latin American, as well as Latinx actors.[9] Finally, as part of a trend towards global production in both North and Latin America, the door was opened for Brazilian director Bruno Barreto and Argentine-Brazilian director Héctor Babenco to develop and produce their films *inside* the industry, with Mexican directors Alfonso Arau (*A Walk in the Clouds*, 1995) and Alfonso Cuarón (*A Little Princess*, 1995), both assisted by Mexican cinematographer Emmanuel "El Chivo" Lubezki, soon to follow.

Viewed from the south, the vectors and genealogies corresponding to this period of engagement are complex. While there has been a growing body of scholarship on the attempts of Hollywood to recruit Latin American talent, to "make sense" of Latin America for U.S. audiences, and to reach out to Latin American film industries and audiences during the Good Neighbor Policy, 1933–1945,[10] Latin Americans' attempts to "make sense" of, capitalize on, parody, and syncretize Hollywood has been critically neglected. In her essay, "Historia nacional, historia transnacional," Ana M. López gives us a conceptual point of departure. In response to the confinement of the study of Latin American cinema on a "continental level" to the New Latin American cinema that emerged in the 1950s and '60s, López proposes resetting the compass to study the vectors of transnational filmmaking by way of "traveling filmmakers" whose mobility includes border crossing within Latin America, as well as in relation to Europe and the United States.[11] Building on this *auteur*-driven, border-crossing model, I propose that we consider how the critical and creative engagement with Hollywood might provide yet another avenue along which to locate important sources of transnational resonance—if not always actual dialogue—among filmmakers and bodies of film practice within Latin America (as exemplified in the historiography of Tunico Amâncio and Marvin D'Lugo),[12] and, just as importantly, the forging of liminal spaces between Latin America and Latinx U.S. for cinematic creation and reception.

Despite the prevailing view voiced by New Latin American filmmakers and theorists, that U.S. cinematic hegemony has interfered profoundly with the development of a Latin American identity in film,[13] I would like to momentarily lift the consideration of economic and political hegemony from the inscription of identity and the conservation of an autochthonous worldview in order to entertain the idea that critical, creative engagement —whether through filmmaking or criticism—can serve as a platform for cultural resilience. In more than one case, creative engagement has coaxed narrative discourse into new arenas of national and social critique; at times, this engagement may even leave its mark *on* Hollywood cinema, such that some hybrid strands (Iñárritu's *The Revenant*, released in 2015 comes to mind) begin to fit what Hamid Naficy has referred to as "accented cinema."[14] To understand how these possibilities of resilience and accentuation have transpired requires—at least *initially*—an unprejudiced openness towards form, genre, national orientation, and even industrial positioning.

AN APPROACH

In essence, the reverse angle, or *contracampo* I am pursuing consists of a parallax view anchored on the one hand in cinephilic memory, the alternate fascination, nostalgia, and melancholy experienced by a Latin American audience that, for decades, has been transnational in imagination and in geographic scope;[15] and on the other, in the real or figurative migration of Latin American filmmakers, actors, and their screen characters towards Los Angeles and the post-systemic studio complex.[16]

During the period under study, this migration became multidirectional: just as the careers and interests of filmmakers such as Suzana Amaral, Helena Solberg, Karim Aïnouz, Salma Hayek, Patricia Cardoso, Arturo Ripstein, Maria Elena Velasco, Alfonso Cuarón, Guillermo del Toro, and Alejandro G. Iñárritu took them northward to shoot

Previous Page: Raúl Juliá and William Hurt in *Kiss of the Spiderwoman* (Héctor Babenco, 1985).

Left: 40th-anniversary commemorative poster for *Memorias del subdesarrollo* (*Memories of Underdevelopment*, Tomás Gutiérrez Alea, 1968).

their films in the United States, other filmmakers such as Nelson Pereira dos Santos, Héctor Babenco, and Raúl Ruiz, went to Europe prior to producing work in the United States. Meanwhile, U.S.-based filmmakers Lourdes Portillo, Gregory Nava, Cheech Marin, Luís Valdez, Robert Rodriguez, and Alex Rivera all found inspiration and a haven for their productions in Mexico. These moves contributed meaningfully to the inscription of a *transfronterizo* or cross-border consciousness in their films, aligning them more closely with a hemispheric, rather than a strictly national audience.

"My family were great moviegoers, and we used to go to the movies all the time and of course [my parents] were always taking home movies . . . so I was surrounded by movies . . . and they were like dreams—

talk about the movie projector being a time machine that captures life, well it's a dream machine . . . I would go into the theater, and the lights would come down, and these images would come up, and they were like dreams . . . I would get caught up in them; they were absolutely marvelous."
— GREGORY NAVA[17]

Latin American filmmakers and film spectators alike can be found on both angles of this parallax view. As avid moviegoers in their youth, several of the filmmakers featured in the Academy Visual History Interviews were profoundly affected by what they saw in Hollywood cinema, albeit as one "foreign" cinema, among others, including European and Asian cinema. How do we assess the influence of "B" movies for Raúl Ruiz, musicals for Héctor

Babenco, Westerns for Nelson Pereira dos Santos and Luís Valdez, epic adventure films for Gregory Nava, Chaplin and Errol Flynn for Lourdes Portillo, Alfred Hitchcock for Arturo Ripstein, horror films for Guillermo del Toro, David Lean and films starring Paul Muni for Edward James Olmos, and so on? The film-going enthusiasm of these filmmakers-in-training invites a consideration of the distance traveled between that "first look" at some point during the 1940s to 1960s and their re-engagement upon mastering the language of filmmaking. It also invites us to consider how Hollywood's Latin American audience has not only influenced, but is often found visibly inscribed within "reverse angle" films, such as José Carlos Burle's *Carnaval Atlântida* (1953), Aïnouz's *Madame Satã* (2002), Suzana Amaral's *A hora da estrela* (*The Hour of the Star*, 1985), Babenco's *Kiss of the Spider Woman* (1985),

Gutiérrez Alea's *Memorias del subdesarrollo* (*Memories of Underdevelopment*, 1968), and Rivera's *Sleep Dealer* (2008). Beyond a presumption of transnational cinephilia, we find in these films a reflexive commentary on the circumstances, manifestations, and possible effects of Hollywood spectatorship.

For example, in *A hora da estrela,* the musings of Macabéa (Marcélia Cartaxo), an orphaned migrant from the Brazilian northeast about Marilyn Monroe, whose skin was the "color of peaches," leads her to dream of becoming a movie star, despite the fact that her self-aggrandizing boyfriend Olímpico (José Dumont) finds her unattractive; she watches movies only in "third-class cinemas because they're much cheaper," and only when she receives her weekly pay.[18] In *Sleep Dealer*, conceived and produced in the digital era, Memo Cruz (Luis Fernando Peña), a young, rural Oaxacan, is a devoted aficionado of "Drones," a show transmitted *via* transborder satellite television. After successfully intercepting the command communications of a drone operator featured on the show, Memo's family home becomes the target of a coordinated U.S. military attack. The act of viewing, whether involving surveillance (by U.S. border agent Rudy Ramírez, played by Jacob Vargas), entertainment, or labor [Luz Martínez' (Leonor Varela) journalism, Memo's work as a Cybracero], becomes an integral part of the protagonists' character arcs as they journey between Oaxaca and Tijuana, San Diego and Oaxaca, *via* Tijuana.

To capture the catalyzing force of cinephilia as well as migration for "reverse angle" cinema, I have organized the remaining discussion according to aesthetic strategy, theme, and the positioning of the spectator, rather than by nationality, filmmaker, or strict chronological sequence. The focus is primarily on narrative fiction filmmaking, rather than documentary, with the caveat that documentary practice informed, coincided with, and helped to shape reverse angle cinema in important ways.

THE 1980S, REVERSE ANGLE

In mainstream Hollywood, the eighties were largely defined by the return of global blockbusters (foreshadowed by Steven Spielberg's *Jaws,* 1975, George Lucas's *Star Wars: Episode IV - A New Hope,* 1977, and Francis Ford Coppola's *Apocalypse Now,* 1979) action adventure films, innovations in sound technology, and computer-generated imagery (CGI), as well as the reemergence (however sporadic) of women's filmmaking (by Bette Gordon, Susan Seidelman, Donna Deitch, Penny Marshall, and Kathryn Bigelow). At the edge of these trends, Latinx directors and actors made sociocultural and aesthetic breakthroughs as part of a "Second Wave" of Latinx filmmaking, by depicting the struggles of Latinxs throughout the twentieth century to gain a foothold in the public sphere, as well as equal treatment and socioeconomic opportunity.[19] As Edward James Olmos explains, in reference to Luís Valdez's *Zoot Suit* (1981, based on the eponymous play), "this is a culture that had been waiting to be heard... With us [the film] was blatantly a story about injustices and profound discrimination, based on truth and reality."[20] At the same time, as Lourdes Portillo has observed, Latinx production in eighties Hollywood was gender bound (all of the directors were male), and in the nineties, most Latina directors were still working on the periphery as independents and in the documentary field.[21]

Within both cinephilic circles and popular discourse, Latin American cinema presented a potent accompaniment to this wave and a new crosscurrent within mainstream filmmaking at large. In addition to the renewed success of Latin American art cinema in Europe (directed by Bruno Barreto, Víctor Gaviria, Ruy Guerra, Raúl Ruiz, and Fernando Solanas) and the first major successes in Anglophone United States and Canada (especially for Héctor Babenco, Paul Leduc, Francisco Lombardi,[22] Héctor Olivera, Luis Puenzo, and Suzana Amaral), there was significant exposure and enthusiasm garnered for this cinema at the San Sebastián Film Festival (Spain), the International Film Festival Rotterdam (Netherlands), and the Sundance, Chicago Latino, and Toronto International Film Festivals.

It should also be noted that to keep up with technical standards in the realm of sound and laboratory processing, many Latin American directors would travel to the United States to use postproduction facilities in New York and Los Angeles, prompting transborder creative-technical collaborations that often remain unpublicized. It was just such a stint, mixing a soundtrack in Los Angeles, which led to Mexican director Arturo Ripstein's meeting with Chicano civil rights activist and labor leader César Chávez, resulting in the documentary short *Tres preguntas a Chávez* (1975).[23]

Following an inverse vector, U.S. Latinx-directed films began screening in Latin America at festivals and in theaters, such as *Zoot Suit* (Colombia, Mexico), *Born in East L.A.* (Brazil, Cuba, Mexico, Peru), *El Norte* (Argentina), and *Stand and Deliver* (Argentina, Brazil, Mexico), while Chicanx and Latinx filmmakers began traveling to Mexico and Argentina to shoot their films. The New Latin American

Far Left: Director and screenwriter Suzana Amaral interviews with Mateus Araujo at her residence in São Paolo, Brazil in 2016, as part of the Academy Visual History Project.

Center Left: Director Alex Rivera talking about his film *Sleep Dealer* (2008) at the Sundance Film Festival.

International Film Festival inaugurated in Havana in 1979, along with the Festival Internacional de Cine de Cartagena de Indias in Colombia, provided vital forums for Latin American filmmakers to share their work, strategize, and undertake co-productions to be launched across the continent. In 1983, Robert M. Young's *The Ballad of Gregorio Cortez* won the Coral Prize and in 1987, Cheech Marin's *Born in East L.A.* received the "Best Script" award at the New Latin American Film Festival in Havana.[24] Some of these festivals have played a critical role in the formation of new generations of Latin American and Latinx filmmakers: the Havana festival provided the impetus for the establishment in 1986 of the International Film and TV School (EICTV) in San Antonio de los Baños, Cuba. The Rotterdam festival became home in 1989 to the Hubert Bals fund, focused on providing production, postproduction, and distribution support to projects developed in Latin America and other economically disadvantaged parts of the world.[25]

Both the Hispanic Decade and the commercial and critical success of Latin American cinema abroad were facilitated by infrastructural changes within hemispheric film industries: on the one hand, the disarticulation of a vertically integrated studio system and the rise of a more horizontal mode of production with independent companies pitching projects to studios for release (in this case, Universal Studios and Warner Brothers) allowed for an increase in ethnic filmmaking (African-American, Asian-American, Latinx) inside the U.S. film industry. Moreover, at a time when Hollywood welcomed the imprint of film-schooled, as well as seasoned American *auteurs*,[26] public television funding and projects such as *American Playhouse* (airing on PBS beginning in 1981) provided a stepping stone for Latinx independent directors and producers such as Gregory Nava, Moctesuma Esparza, and later, Severo Pérez, to get their feature films produced and exhibited theatrically, as well as on the small screen.[27] Meanwhile, state-funded film agencies in Latin America, such as Embrafilme (Brazil), IMCINE (Mexico), and the INC (Argentina) stepped up their sponsorship of screenings at foreign film festivals, and provided national filmmakers with co-production funding, significantly increasing the international heft and visibility of Latin American art cinema. The presence, by the mid-eighties of exile communities, including filmmakers, in North America and Europe also created a small, but vocal audience for production in exile and the diffusion of Latin American co-productions.

Within national cinemas, profound political and economic changes linked to the end of military rule across Latin America (with the notable exceptions of Guatemala, Paraguay, and Uruguay) sparked new social themes and a referencing of the international political sphere, even as domestic cultural scenes were being reshaped by an explicit, institutionally transformative move towards greater participation and inclusion of marginalized populations. For example, the Brazilian centennial of the abolition of slavery in 1988 prompted the production and release of the first Afro-Brazilian-directed feature, Zózimo Bulbul's *Abolição* (1988), and an ensuing wave of work addressing Afro-Brazilian history and identity stretching into the new millennium such as Carlos Diegues' *Orfeu* (1999), Sergio Bianchi's *Quanto vale ou é por quilo?* (*What Is It Worth?*, 2005), and Tata Amaral's *Antônia* (2006). In the late 1980s, for the first time, an Afro-Brazilian woman proudly hailing from a Rio de Janeiro *favela* was democratically elected to Congress; an achievement documented in Eunice Gutman's eponymous film *Benedita da Silva* (1990).

Directors of many politically charged films[28] availed themselves of the political opening to reveal the human face of violence and repression perpetrated under recent military rule and the lasting damage to civil society. Several of these films addressed this topic obliquely, by delving back into earlier periods of state repression, such as the Estado Nôvo[29] (Brazil) and World War II (Argentina), as if to point to the need for a redefinition of, rather than a simple "return" to, democratic rule.

As part of this political opening, there was a searching inquiry into, and contestation of, patriarchal power, that allowed for a queer turn in Latin American cinema, which, in substance, and with two or three exceptions,[30] anticipated the open,

non-stereotypical representation of queer life and identity in U.S. cinema in the early nineties. As in Brazil, where stars such as Grande Otelo had performed in drag as part of the carnivalesque inversions characteristic of *chanchadas* (musical comedies), drag performance was occasionally evident in the urban comedies of Cantinflas and Tin Tan, and it was revived with the popularity of the *fichera* or prostitute-centered erotic comedies of the seventies.[31] Then towards the end of the seventies, Mexican filmmaker Arturo Ripstein took the theme of homosexuality out of a subcultural status and into the national and international limelight with *El lugar sin límites* (*The Place Without Limits*, 1978), based on a short story by José Donoso and scripted in collaboration with Manuel Puig.

Left: Daniel Stern and Cheech Marin in *Born in East L.A.*, 1987 Right: Director Carlos Diegues interviews with Lúcia Nagib at the Hôtel Bel Ami in Paris in 2016, as part of the Academy Oral History Project.

The social impact of Ripstein's film derives from its tapping of the *fichera* film for ambience and characterization, coupled with its use of visual construction and character development to allow the focalization of the plot through La Manuela, a transwoman prostitute played by Roberto Cobo (El Jaibo in Luis Buñuel's *Los olvidados*, 1950) and her daughter Japonesita (Ana Martín). By portraying the manner by which La Manuela's brothel is patronized by small town patriarch Don Alejo (Fernando Soler) and a self-conflicted, homo-curious client, Pancho (Gonzalo Vega), Ripstein is able to lay bare deeply rooted contradictions and pave the way for a free, if momentary (the film ends

tragically), exploration of sexuality in relation to modern subjectivity, queer family, as well as the chronic discrimination and violence stemming from homophobia.

The fixity of social boundaries imposed by traditional concepts of gender and sexuality was challenged further in two films that opened the possibility for constructive dialogue between heterosexual and homosexual men. The close friendships formed in Babenco's *Kiss of the Spider Woman* (based on the eponymous novel by Manuel Puig) and *Fresa y chocolate* (*Strawberry and Chocolate* Tomás Gutiérrez Alea, 1993) between prisoners Molina, arrested for child

molestation (William Hurt) and Arregui, a political prisoner of the Dirty War under military rule (Raúl Juliá); and the gay art collector Diego (Jorge Perugorría) and young revolutionary student David (Vladimir Cruz) respectively, forge a promising—if fragile—terrain for deconstructing stereotypes attached to the revolutionary left, as well as queer subjectivity. By exposing and assuaging homophobic fear along with internal resistance to tolerance, and by cultivating empathy and solidarity among historically conflicted sectors of society (a conflict that is shown to be exploited by the State), Babenco and Gutiérrez Alea each provide nuanced, humanistic responses to the controversy generated by the release of Néstor Almendros and Orlando Jiménez Leal's documentary *Improper Conduct* (1984), which denounced the mistreatment of homosexuals under the Castro government in Cuba in the mid-1960s. *Kiss of the Spider Woman* reportedly grossed over $16 million at the box-office during its first year of U.S. release, whereas *Strawberry and Chocolate* screened at Sundance and brought in over $2 million after a more modest theatrical run. Both films were nominated for Oscars, with the former winning Best Actor for William Hurt and Best Picture for producer David Weisman.[32] The considerable commercial and critical success of these films in the United States can be seen as helping to turn the tide towards inclusion of queer perspectives in U.S. commercial cinema and television (Jonathan Demme, Todd Haynes, Donna Deitch), as well as the commercial release of films by Latin American directors in the United States.

Meanwhile, access to film schools and the formation of feminist film collectives (often intersecting with broader social movements) in Brazil, Chile, Colombia, and Mexico, helped launch a new generation of women filmmakers and screenwriters who tried their hand at fiction filmmaking. María Luisa

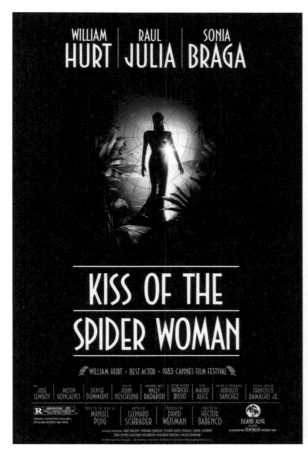

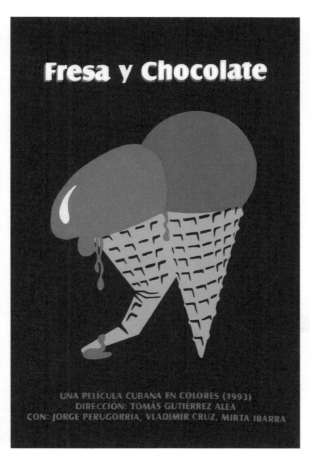

Mothers of the Plaza de Mayo (1985), a labor of love and admiration for the courageous Madres, which provided an enduring and well-rounded factual complement to the melodramatic fiction, *La historia oficial* (*The Official Story, 1985*) directed by Luis Puenzo and co-scripted by Aída Bortnik, released later the same year. As Lourdes Portillo explains,

Bemberg (Argentina), Aída Bortnik (screenwriter, Argentina), Bertha Navarro (producer, Mexico & U.S.), Paz Alicia Garcíadiego (screenwriter, Mexico), Busi Cortés, María Novaro, and Maryse Sistach (Mexico), Suzana Amaral and Tizuka Yamasaki (Brazil), and Marilda Vera and Fina Torres (Venezuela) each were able to complete their first feature films during the 1980s,[33] receiving a boost in distribution from international film festival venues, such as the Films de Femmes Festival in Créteil, France, and

transnational feminist networks (especially in France, Spain, the Netherlands, and the U.S.).[34] Women documentary makers, many of whom worked initially within collectives, began to rely on Canada's Studio D and women's health and human rights NGOs for production funding and distribution support. It was within this receptive, awakened climate that Chicana filmmaker Lourdes Portillo collaborated with Argentine émigré Susana Blaustein Muñoz to direct the Oscar-nominated documentary, *Las Madres: The*

Finally, the audience for Latin American and Latinx cinema was beginning to grow outward geographically, and diversify within national boundaries. The availability of low-cost video production and changes to national audiovisual legislation in Bolivia, Brazil, and Colombia, dovetailed with growing grassroots cultural networks to generate niche-audiences for community-level productions, including indigenous media, films about the AIDS crisis, reproductive health, daily life in *arrabales* and *favelas* (urban slums).[36] Notwithstanding the political opening in the Southern Cone, severe debt crises in Argentina, Mexico, and Brazil, combined with armed conflict and counter-insurgency efforts in Guatemala, Nicaragua, and El Salvador prompted an upsurge in the migrant stream northward to Japan, the United States, and Europe, as documented in films by Lourdes Portillo and Nina Serrano (*After the Earthquake*, 1979), Jorge and Mabel Preloran (*Zulay Facing the 21ˢᵗ Century*, 1989), Tânia Cypriano (*Grandma Has a Video Camera*, 2007), Martin Lucas (*Guatemala: A Journey to the End of Memories*, 1986),

and Olivia Carrescia (*Todos santos,* [*The Survivors*, 1989], *Mayan Voices, American Lives,* 1994). In contrast with previous decades, not only was the number of foreign-born on the rise in the U.S. (from 9.6 million in 1970 to 19.8 million in 1990)[37] but the share of Latin Americans—especially of Mexicans and Central Americans—as part of that immigration increased exponentially.[38] An expanding Latin American diasporic audience in the United States found social and cultural recognition in Golden Age Mexican classics still showing in urban repertory theaters, as well as in low-budget Hispanophone, hybrid genre films (*churros*) depicting the cross-border migrant experience.

Many of these *churros* were produced by independent companies located near the U.S.-Mexico border and were distributed on videotape at local businesses and viewed on Spanish-language television, in addition to neighborhood theaters.[39] In a scene from María Elena Velasco's *Ni de aquí, ni de allá* (1986), when María in the persona of "La India María" is adrift in Los Angeles, she walks by the marquee of a downtown movie palace advertising a performance by Vicente Fernández as well as "La India María," encapsulating the notion that migration can somehow lead to stardom, even if it is confined to one's linguistic and national diasporic community. The fearlessness and ingenuity with which popular female performers such as Velasco and Rosa Gloria Chagoyán (*aka* "Lola la Trailera") crossed the border into recondite realms of Anglo wealth and power in these low-budget films gave shape to a potent form of vernacular feminism on the Mexican transnational screen that appealed to multi-gendered Latinx audiences.

Prior to the 1980s, the representation of Latinx Los Angeles in Anglo-directed sound era films was exceedingly rare—Archie Mayo's *Bordertown* (1935), and Michael Pressman's *Boulevard Nights* (1979) are among the exceptions. An important accomplishment of the Hispanic Decade was to bring the local community to life on the big screen, either by design, as in Valdez's *Zoot Suit,* (1981), and Artenstein's *Break of Dawn,* (1988), or by taking crews on location in Boyle Heights and East L.A. to provide the settings for films such as *Born in East L.A.*, *El Norte, Stand and Deliver,* and *American Me* (Edward James Olmos, 1992). These projects underscore how the depiction and recognition of socio-culturally meaningful places in film can be as appealing to Latinx moviegoers as the casting of Latinx actors. As Edward James Olmos reveals in his Academy Visual History Interview, these phenomena are interrelated: the casting of an Angelino, Olmos, in *Zoot Suit,* a film about the Sleepy Lagoon arrests of young East Los Angeles Mexican-Americans in 1942, greatly enhanced the portrayal of the Pachuco character as a "Greek chorus, the voice, the alter ego, the essence of the plot, the real storyteller" of the film.[40] Conversely, the legacy of the Latinx presence in U.S. film became visually inscribed in the space of the city itself as part of a growing mural movement: in 1985, Latinx artist Eloy Torrez painted a giant portrait of Mexican-American film star Anthony Quinn, popularly titled "The Pope of Broadway" on the side of the Victor Clothing building on South Broadway, not far from a string of movie palaces that had long been popular among Latinxs.[41]

DESTINATION: NUESTRA SEÑORA LA REINA DE LOS ÁNGELES DE PORCIÚNCULA

In Gregory Nava's *El Norte*, Guatemalan newcomer Rosa (Zaide Silvia Gutiérrez) and seasoned Mexican migrant Nacha (Lupe Ontiveros) contemplate the cityscape after escaping from a raid on a downtown factory:

"Nacha, do you know where the gringos live? Just look at the street! It looks like Mexico!"

"For God's sake, you don't think the gringos are going to want to live with Mexicans, do you? They live over there in their neighborhoods."

Significantly, the films of the Hispanic Decade combatted the potential ghettoization of Latinx communities by foregrounding the dynamic, if often tense, relationship between migrants and Anglo and Chicanx Angelinos. Just as migration from Mexico was on the rise, so were deportations under the new Simpson-Mazzoli Act of 1986. In Latinx comedies and melodramas crafting realist portrayals of immigrant experience, the anxiety around workplace raids is palpable; it propels the plot of *Born in East L.A.* as Angelino Chicano Rudy (Cheech Marin) is rounded up by mistake in a *peluche* factory and deported to Tijuana, and it triggers turning points in the professional fates of Guatemalan refugees Rosa and her brother Enrique (David Villalpando) in *El Norte*, who risk deportation in raids on a garment factory and a high-end restaurant, respectively. It also figures as an allegorical referent in Artenstein's *Break of Dawn*, which depicts the tenuousness of citizenship for Mexican-American Angelinos, many of whom were deported in 1930s raids. The dystopian dimension of migration—the policing of urban space, the attempt to disguise one's national origin, the difficulties gaining acceptance into the native-born community—is also cultivated in a growing body of Mexican films that follow migrants to Los Angeles. Unlike earlier Mexican films produced during the Bracero Program such as Alejandro Galindo's *Espaldas mojadas* (1955), these films, which paralleled the attention of Mexican policymakers and print media to the effects

of emigration,[42] opened up a space for feminine protagonism and social agency. In Arturo Ripstein's *La ilegal* (1979), an unwed pregnant woman, Claudia (Lucía Méndez) travels to Los Angeles to join the father of her child, Felipe (Pedro Armendáriz, Jr.), a successful businessman who is already married to someone else. Claudia gives birth, and is sheltered by Felipe in a Malibu bungalow until she is framed by his jealous wife for pornographic activity, and deported. Like Ripstein's other characters, Claudia struggles to return—this time crossing the river—to be reunited with her child. In the carnivalesque *Ni de aquí, ni de allá*, directed by María Elena Velasco, a young indigenous woman, María (Velasco) agrees to migrate with an L.A.-bound U.S. couple the Wilsons, to work as their factotum to help her father purchase a tractor for their small farm. After being separated from the Wilsons by customs agents at LAX, María becomes embroiled in an FBI hunt for an international crime ring and is also pursued by a Soviet spy. As she takes on various jobs, her upward mobility is compromised by her assertion of her ethnic identity and her technophobia, and after escaping from an INS raid at El Coyote restaurant, a humiliating stint as a giant hen, and mishaps with the hyper-technologized sickbed of an elderly millionaire she cares for, she is deported, but not without taking a few gadgets as souvenirs back to Mexico.

During the 1980s, the Anglo audience for Latin American and Latinx cinema was changing as well: movements in solidarity with exile communities and the civilian opposition to military rule in the Southern Cone provided a captive activist and academic market for the distribution of the above-mentioned feature films and documentaries,

Left: Poster for
Tonta tonta, pero no tanto
(Fernando Cortés, 1972).

while the fortified appearance on Anglo television and in Hollywood films of Latinx actors (Alfonso Arau, Sonia Braga, Edward James Olmos, Lupe Ontiveros) and the resurgent marketing of Ibero-American culture as sensual and spicy thanks to filmmakers Pedro Almodóvar (Spain) and Bruno Barreto (*Dona Flor e seus dois maridos*, 1976), lured Latinx-curious Anglophone middle-class viewers towards feature films exhibited in urban art theaters and occasionally, suburban venues. The latter trend reached its peak with the pairing of traditional Mexican cuisine and young adult passion in *Como agua para chocolate* (Alfonso Arau, 1992), which, after reaching over 170 theaters in 1993, became the "highest-grossing Spanish-language import of all time."[43]

The success of these actors and films was also due, in large part, to the captive Latinx audience for Hollywood films: a 1997 study of the Latinx audience in California revealed that a large majority of U.S.-born Latinxs (88.8%) watched movies in theaters, and nationally Latinxs spent over $10 billion on entertainment that year, and the largest share of their entertainment income (6.5%) on movie admissions, compared to other ethnic groups.[44] And in 2012, although they constituted only 18 percent of the movie-going audience, Latinxs purchased 25 percent of all movie tickets sold.[45]

The impact of this period of re-democratization, decentering of production in Mexico, transnational migration, and tapping of diasporic audiences on production strategy, thematics, casting, and film style should not be underestimated. On the one hand, as Mary Beltrán has observed, "shifts in the dominant racial paradigms that guided casting and star promotion began to be evident in the Hollywood star system"[46] in the eighties and in the attempt to address emerging markets, Latinx audiovisual expression ran

the gamut from independent experimental and documentary films to low-budget features to national cinema imports (from Latin America), Latinx exports (to Latin America), to international co-productions destined for a broader global market. On the other hand, there is ample evidence that Latinx actors still faced barriers to obtaining meaningful roles outside of Latinx productions. In the early nineties, Luís Valdez observed that the Hollywood power structure still showed "a lack of courage and confidence that a Latino film can get out there and reach a broad audience," and lamented the lack of clout on the part of Hispanic advocacy organizations to chisel through this barrier.[47] Just as importantly, the rebooting of industrial cinema and the geo-cultural expansion of box office success raised the old questions, once again, of film language and targeted audience. Were successful Latin American filmmakers "watering down" film aesthetics and popularizing politics in favor of a broader, international audience? Could these new, more polished, occasionally star- or soon-to-be-star-driven films, some directed by former Cinema Novo and Grupo Cine Liberación directors, still be considered "New Latin American Cinema"?[48] For whom and by whom was this global trend being propelled?

QUESTIONS FOR FUTURE THOUGHT

"Latin American filmmakers have some things to offer their North American counterparts, particularly in these critical times when funding seems to be drying up, when

television programmers fall prey to intimidation tactics, and filmmakers fear a return to the blacklist . . . Maybe the solution is to approach certain topics less directly, to find other ways of saying things. This is where Latin American filmmakers offer a particularly useful set of examples, having developed ways of communicating under the harshest kinds of censorship and repression." – HELENA SOLBERG[49]

There is no simple answer to the questions posed above; for although there was a marked improvement in production values in the eighties (with the exception of the low-budget border *churros*), in substantive terms, filmmakers continued to favor stylistic and generic hybridity, drawing on the montage aesthetics, grotesque realism,[50] neorealist strategies, and the carnivalesque as tools for representing contemporary reality, reveling in parody, and evoking the suffering brought on by military rule, the disenfranchisement and humiliating treatment experienced during migration. Importantly, this hybridity provided an aesthetic correlate for character (and by extension, spectator) ambivalence towards national modernity and global capitalism. A strong attempt to link marginal identities to the changing definition of citizenship included the process whereby the filmmakers drew on their roots and relationship to place for inspiration: in their Academy Visual History Interviews, the places where Nava, Valdez, Olmos, Marin, and Portillo first encountered the cinema and Anglo society inflected their respective approaches to representation and narration as Latinx directors, while both Babenco and Ripstein discuss how their lives were shaped by being Jewish in Latin America, with Babenco experiencing exile in Spain and Ripstein making *El santo oficio* (*The Holy Inquisition*, 1974) in order to revisit the Mexican Inquisition from a Jewish perspective.[51]

In this essay, I have made a historically specific inquiry into the relationship between Hollywood and Latin American cinemas to look beyond a pattern of decades-long dominance to reveal a series of complex interactions from apprenticeship (Nelson Pereira dos Santos), to co-production (Héctor Babenco), to collaboration (Bertha Navarro and Gregory Nava), to distribution (Ramón Menéndez, Warner Brothers, Tomás Gutiérrez Alea, Miramax), to parody (Burle, Sganzerla), to performance space (Braga, Olmos), and fandom (Amaral, Babenco, and Aïnouz). These differential positionings and modes of engagement have helped to produce "reverse angles" from which Latin American and Latinx filmmakers could launch their creative expressions across geo-cultural boundaries, reach new audiences, and find a platform for transnational authorship. In the process, they created a hybrid, interstitial audiovisual space within which to begin to view and rethink the encounter between Latin America and Latinx U.S. differently.

The recent directing opportunities in the industry for Latin American filmmakers, from the Three Amigos (Cuarón, Iñarrítu, and del Toro) Patricia Riggen to Eugenio Derbez to Diego Luna and Pablo Larraín, along with initiatives by the Academy of Motion Picture Arts and Sciences itself to diversify its membership, lead us to consider whether the industry is finally becoming a space within which Latinx visions can be inscribed in authorial terms, forming the possibility for diverse, diasporic viewers to experience the recognition they have long sought, hoped for, and deserved.

DR. CATHERINE L. BENAMOU
Associate Professor of Film and Media Studies and Visual Studies,
University of California, Irvine

Dr. Benamou is the author of *It's All True: Orson Welles's Pan-American Odyssey* (University of California Press, 2007), which is one of the most comprehensive studies on Welles's sojourn in Brazil and Latin America. Her research on Latin American and Latinix Cinema and Media focuses on authorial itineraries, documentary, media ethnography and historiography, with an emphasis on media cultures and the hemispheric politics and aesthetics of the Americas. She has received the National Endowment of the Humanities Fellowship for a book she is writing on transnational television and its reception by diasporic Latinx audiences. She serves on the editorial boards of *Framework*, *DOC Online*, *REBECA*, *Mediático*, and the *Catalán Journal of Communication and Cultural Studies*, and contributes as consultant to the Orson Welles Archive at the University of Michigan-Ann Arbor. She received her Ph.D. in Cinema Studies from New York University.

Left: Gael García Bernal,
Antonia Zegers, and Pablo Larraín
on the Oscars red carpet, 2013.

NOTES

1. The terminology used to designate people of Latin American descent in the United States has undergone a series of evolutions to reflect a gender balance (Latina/o, Latin@), and most recently, gender neutrality, which is indicated by "Latinx."

2. See Seth Fein, "From Collaboration to Containment: Hollywood and the International Political Economy of Mexican Cinema after the Second World War," in *Mexico's Cinema: A Century of Film and Filmmakers,* eds. Joanne Hershfield and David R. Maciel (Wilmington: Scholarly Resources, 1999), 148–152; Randal Johnson, *The Film Industry in Brazil* (Pittsburgh: University of Pittsburgh Press, 1987), 34–40, 134–36, 179–183; Randal Johnson and Robert Stam, "The Shape of Brazilian Film History," in *Brazilian Cinema*, expanded edition, eds. Randal Johnson and Robert Stam (New York: Columbia University Press, 1995), 22–23, 27–29; Arnaldo Jabor, "Jack Valenti's Brazilian Agenda," in *Brazilian Cinema*, eds. Randal Johnson and Robert Stam, 109–114; Toby Miller, "Hollywood History, Cultural Imperialism, and Globalisation," in Toby Miller et al., *Global Hollywood* (London: British Film Institute, 2001), 17–28, 34–41; Francisco Peredo Castro, *Cine y propaganda para Latinoamérica, México y Estados Unidos en la encrucijada de los años cuarenta* (México, D.F.: Universidad Nacional Autónoma de México, Centro de Investigaciones sobre América del Norte: Centro Coordinador y Difusor de Estudios Latinoamericanos, 2004), 291–321, 332–354: and Tamara Falicov, "Hollywood's Presence in Latin America: Production Participation to Distribution Dominance," in *Blackwell's International Encyclopedia of Media Studies*, Vol. II, "Media Production," ed. Vicki Mayer (Malden, MA: Wiley-Blackwell Publishers, 2013), 255–276.

3. See, for example, the essays and manifestoes by Glauber Rocha, Fernando Solanas and Octavio Getino, Julio García Espinosa, and Fernando Birri in *New Latin American Cinema: Theory, Practices, and Continental Articulations,* vol. I, ed. Michael T. Martin (Detroit: Wayne State University Press, 1997); and Jorge Sanjinés, "Language and Popular Culture," trans. John King, in Coco Fusco ed., *Reviewing Histories: Selections from New Latin American Cinema* (Buffalo: Hallwalls Contemporary Arts Center, 1987), 156–163.

4. This is exemplified in the work of Raúl Ruiz and Miguel Littín in Chile, Paul Leduc and Arturo Ripstein in Mexico, Nelson Pereira dos Santos, Ruy Guerra, and Glauber Rocha in Brazil, Julio García Espinosa, Sara Gomez, and Tomás Gutiérrez Alea in Cuba, Jorge Sanjinés in Bolivia, and Raymundo Gleyzer and Fernando Ayala in Argentina. Not included in this list is the vitally important documentary work—during this same period—of Fernando Birri (Argentina), Eduardo Coutinho (Brazil), Santiago Alvarez (Cuba), and Patricio Guzmán (Chile).

5. In her essay "Historia nacional, historia transnacional,"Ana M. López applied the concept of "contact zone," introduced by literary scholar Mary Louise Pratt, to underscore the transnational exchanges that have occurred during the building of national cinemas in Latin America; Ana M. López, "Historia nacional, historia transnacional," in *Horizontes del segundo siglo: Investigación y pedagogía del cine mexicano, latinoamericano y chicano*, eds. Julianne Burton-Carvajal, Patricia Torres San Martín, and Ángel Miquel (Guadalajara: Universidad de Guadalajara/Instituto Mexicano de Cinematografía, 1998), 77; here, I am relocating and reapplying it to focus on Latin American filmmakers' practical and conceptual exchanges with the U.S. industry.

6. The first period of Latin American participation in the industry was during the transition to sound; see the essay by Cari Beauchamp in this volume.

7. Sadly, many of these theaters would close during the 1990s with the advent of consumer-friendly videotape, DVDs, and digital theatrical projection.

8. These include Luís Valdez (*Zoot Suit,* 1981, *La Bamba*, 1985), Gregory Nava (*El Norte*, 1983), León Ichaso (*Crossover Dreams*, 1985), Cheech Marin (*Born in East LA*, 1987), Ramón Menéndez (*Stand and Deliver*, 1988), Isaac Artenstein (*Break of Dawn*, 1988), as well as Latinx-oriented films by like-minded Anglo directors (Robert M. Young and Robert Redford).

9. Including, Sonia Braga (Brazil), Edward James Olmos (U.S.), Tony Plana (Cuban-American), Pepe Serna (U.S.), Esai Morales U.S.), Elizabeth Peña, María Rojo (Mexico), Cheech Marin, Rubén Blades, Andy García, Lupe Ontiveros, and Ernesto Gómez Cruz (Mexico).

10. See, for example, the analyses and historical background provided in Catherine L. Benamou, *It's All True: Orson Welles's Pan-American Odyssey* (Berkeley: University of California Press, 2007), Gisela Cramer and Ursula Prutsch, eds., *¡Américas Unidas!, Nelson A. Rockefeller's Office of Inter-American Affairs* (Madrid: Iberoamericana; Frankfurt: Vervuert, 2012); Marvin D'Lugo, "Aural Identity, Genealogies of Sound Technologies, and Hispanic Transnationality on Screen," in *World Cinemas, Transnational Perspectives*, ed. Nataša Ďurovičová and Kathleen Newman (New York: Routledge, 2010), 160–185; Ana M. López, "Are All Latins from Manhattan? Hollywood Ethnography and Cultural Colonialism" in *Mediating Two Worlds: Cinematic Encounters in the Americas*, eds. John King, Ana M. López, and Manuel Alvarado (London: British Film Institute, 1993), 67–80; and Ana Rita Mendonça, *Carmen Miranda foi a Washington* (Rio de Janeiro: Editora Record, 1999).

11. López, "Historia nacional, historia transnacional," 75, 77–78. Unless otherwise indicated, all translations from Spanish and Portuguese are my 6wn.

12. See Tunico Amâncio, "Fuzuê em Gaza (Poder, corpos e humor)" in *Brasil-México: aproximações cinematográficas*, eds. Tunico Amâncio and Marina Cavalcanti Tedesco (Niterói, RJ: Editora da Universidade Federal Fluminense, 2011), 37–51; and D'Lugo, "Aural Identity, Genealogies of Sound Technologies, and Hispanic Transnationality on Screen."

13. See, for example, Fernanda Solórzano, "Interview with Arturo Ripstein: No Contest," trans. Daynalí Flores Rodríguez, *Discourse: Journal for Theoretical Studies in Media and Culture* 26, nos. 1 and 2 (2004): 47, Fernando Solanas and Octavio Getino, "Towards a Third Cinema," in *New Latin American Cinema* vol. I, ed. Michael T. Martin (Detroit: Wayne State University Press, 1997), 41–42, and Tomás Gutiérrez Alea, "The Viewer's Dialectic," 112.

14. Accented cinema, usually produced by filmmakers who have experienced geo-cultural displacement, has been described as "one of the offshoots of Third Cinema . . . Like the *Hour of the Furnaces* [directed by Fernando Solanas and Octavio Getino], accented films are hybridized in their use of forms that cut across the national, typological, generic, and stylistic boundaries," in Hamid Naficy, *An Accented Cinema: Exilic and Diasporic Filmmaking* (Princeton: Princeton University Press, 2001), 30–31.

Left: Cheech Marin in a scene from *Born in East L.A.,* 1987.

15. Recent scholarship has underscored the significance of Latin American diasporic audiences for Spanish-language cinema in the United States dating as far back as the 1910s; see Colin Gunckel, *Mexico on Main Street: Transnational Film Culture in Los Angeles Before World War II* (New Brunswick: Rutgers University Press, 2015); Robert McKee Irwin, "Mexican National Cinema in the USA: Good Neighbours and Transnational Mexican Audiences," in *Global Mexican Cinema: its Golden Age*, eds. Robert McKee Irwin and Maricruz Castro Ricalde (London: BFI/Palgrave Macmillan, 2013); Toby Miller, "National Cinema Abroad: The New International Division of Cultural Labor, From Production to Viewing," in *World Cinemas, Transnational Perspectives*, eds. Nataša Ďurovičová and Kathleen Newman (New York: Routledge, 2010), 144–48; and Laura Isabel Serna, *Making Cinelandia: American Films and Mexican Film Culture Before the Golden Age* (Durham: Duke University Press 2014).

16. My approach here is in partial alignment with the observation by Brazilian film scholar Paulo Antônio Paranaguá that "in Latin American societies, the only permanent relationship with film is that of reception," and therefore any effort at periodization of the cinema in that region should be "based on the evolution of film audiences" in Paulo Antônio Paranaguá, "Of Periodizations and Paradigms: The Fifties in Comparative Perspective," *Nuevo Texto Crítico* 11, nos. 21/22 (1998): 32.

17. Academy Visual History with Gregory Nava, interviewed by Lourdes Portillo in Beverly Hills, June 16, 2015. Henceforth referred to simply as "Academy Visual History Interview."

18. From dialogue between Macabéa and Olímpico in Clarice Lispector, *The Hour of the Star*, trans. Giovanni Pontiero (New York: New Directions Publishing, 1992), 53. The same dialogue is reproduced in the eponymous film.

19. The Hispanic Decade was an important part of this wave. I am in agreement here with the periodization offered by Charles Ramírez Berg, who states in his book *Latino Images in Film* that there was a "Second Wave" of Chicano cinema beginning in 1977, the year Robert M. Young's *¡Alambrista!* was released; see Ramírez Berg, *Latino Images in Film* 186–87; for more on the Hispanic Decade, see Rosa-Linda Fregoso, *The Bronze Screen: Chicana and Chicano Film Culture* (Minneapolis, MN: University of Minnesota Press, 1993); Charles Ramírez Berg, *Latino Images in Film* (Austin: University of Texas Press, 2002), 185–189; and Chon A. Noriega, ed., *Chicanos and Film: Representation and Resistance* (Minneapolis, MN: University of Minnesota Press, 1992).

20. Academy Visual History with Edward James Olmos, interviewed by Lourdes Portillo in Encino, May 15, 2014.

21. Lourdes Portillo, "On Chicanas and Filmmaking: A Commentary," in *Chicana (W)rites on Word and Film*, ed. María Helena Herrera-Sobek and Helena María Viramontes (Berkeley: Third Woman Press, 1995), 281.

22. For more on the late twentieth-century Peruvian boom, including *La boca del lobo* (Francisco Lombardi, 1988), see Jeffrey Middents, *Hablemos de Cine: Film Journals and Film Culture in Peru* (Hanover, NH: University Press of New England, 2009).

23. An experience described in Academy Visual History with Arturo Ripstein, interviewed by Lourdes Portillo in Mexico City, September 23, 2015.

24. Fregoso, *The Bronze Screen*, 55.

25. The EICTV school was founded by Nobel Prize-winning Colombian author Gabriel García Márquez and a group of Argentine, Brazilian, and Cuban filmmakers. For more information on each of these incubators, see Escuela Internacional de Cine y Televisión, Escuela de Cine en San Antonio de los Baños, Cuba, accessed December 21, 2016, http://www.eictv.org, and "About HBF/IFFR," Hubert Bals Fund, Rotterdam International Film Festival, accessed December 32, 2016, https://iffr.com/en/professionals/iffr-industry/hubert-bals-fund/about-hbf, respectively.

26. Woody Allen, Clint Eastwood, Stanley Kubrick, Spike Lee, George Lucas, Martin Scorsese, Steven Spielberg, and Luís Valdez.

27. Severo Pérez directed *...And the Earth Did Not Swallow Him* for *American Playhouse* in 1995. See Academy Visual History with Gregory Nava, interviewed by Lourdes Portillo in Beverly Hills, June 16, 2015, for details on the production history of *El Norte* (1984).

28. Directors and films include: *Pobre mariposa* (*Poor Butterfly*, Raúl de la Torre, Argentina, 1986), *La historia oficial* (The Official Story, Luis Puenzo, Argentina, 1985), *Sur* (*The South*, Fernando E. Solanas, Argentina, 1988), *Eles não usam black-tie.* (They Don't Wear Black Tie, Leon Hirszman, Brazil, 1981), *Memórias do cárcere* (*Memoirs of Prison*, Nelson Pereira dos Santos, Brazil, 1984), *Pra frente, Brasil* (Go Ahead, Brazil!, Roberto Farias, Brazil, 1982), *Patriamada* (*Beloved Country Brazil*, Tizuka Yamasaki, Brazil, 1984), *Kiss of the Spiderwoman* (Héctor Babenco, Brazil/U.S., 1985), *Sonho de valsa* (*Dream Waltz*, Ana Carolina, Brazil, 1987), and *Mémoire des apparences* (*Life Is a Dream*, Raúl Ruiz, France 1987).

29. The Estado Nôvo, or "New State," was a period of authoritarian rule in Brazil under populist dictator Getúlio Vargas, from 1937 to 1945. It involved strict censorship, control of communications media, central state control of labor unions, the outlaw of Afro-Brazilian religion, and the repression of leftist political opposition, depicted in Nelson Pereira dos Santos's film *Memórias do cárcere*.

30. *The Boys in the Band* (William Friedkin, 1970), a low-budget studio film, *Norman...Is That You?* (George Schlatter, 1976), starring Redd Foxx, Pearl Baily, and Michael Warren, and the indie film *Desert Hearts* (Donna Deitch, 1985), stand in notable exception to the dominant, normalizing discourse of the "temporary transvestite" film; for a discussion of the latter, see Chris Straayer, *Deviant Eyes, Deviant Bodies: Sexual Re-Orientation in Film and Video* (New York: Columbia University Press, 1996). I am indebted to my colleague Lucas Hilderbrand for his insights regarding the history of trans-representation in U.S. cinema during this period.

31. See Sergio de la Mora, *Cinemachismo: Masculinities and Sexuality in Mexican Film* (Austin, TX: University of Texas Press, 2006) for an in-depth critical assessment of the *fichera* film.

32. For *Kiss of the Spider Woman*, see [no author], "Island Exex Slated for IFPW Seminar," *Variety* May 21, 1986, Clippings File, Margaret Herrick Library, Academy of Motion Picture Arts and Sciences, Los Angeles; for *Strawberry and Chocolate*, see "Box Office/Business for Strawberry and Chocolate," imdb.com, http://www.imdb.com/title/tt0106966/business?ref_=ttfc_sa_3, accessed February 19, 2017.

33. See Academy Visual History Interviews for Bertha Navarro, Paz Alicia Garcíadiego, María Novaro, and Suzana Amaral for details regarding the production of these projects.

34. Of note is the *Punto de Vista: Latina* project at Women Make Movies, Inc. which provided an exhibition and distribution platform for films by Latin American women directors; see Catherine L. Benamou and Bienvenida Matías, "Remembering *Punto de Vista: Latina* in Two Voices," *Camera Obscura* 28, no. 1 (2013): 133–145.

35. Academy Visual History with Lourdes Portillo, interviewed by Sienna McLean-LoGreco in Hollywood, December 5, 2013.

36. For examples of these productions, see Alexander Street Press, Canal Futura, Cine-Ojo, and Camila Films, *Latin America in Video* (Alexandria, VA: Alexander Street Press, 2014).

37. See the graph in Alejandro Portes and Rubén G. Rumbaut, *Immigrant America, A Portrait*, 4th ed. (Berkeley: University of California Press, 2014), 25.

38. By 1990, Hispanics accounted for 9% of the total population, and 25% of the population in California. See Table 2, "Población Hispana por Origen para Regiones, Estados y Puerto Rico: 1990 y 2000," in Betsy Guzmán, *Población Hispana, Información del Censo 2000* (Washington, D.C.: U.S. Census Bureau, U.S. Department of Commerce, Economics and Statistics Administration, 2001), 4.

39. For information on low-budget Mexican border productions, see Adán Ávalos, "The Naco in Mexican Film: La banda del carro rojo, Border Cinema, and Migrant Audiences," in Latsploitation, Exploitation Cinemas, and Latin America, ed. Victoria Ruétalo and Dolores Tierney (New York: Routledge, 2009), 190–194, and Norma Iglesias, "Reconstructing the Border: Mexican Border Cinema and its Relationship to its Audience," in *Mexico's Cinema, A Century of Filmmakers*, ed. Joanne Hershfield and David R. Maciel, 233–235. Charles Ramírez Berg mentions that although there were more than 250 Spanish-language theaters in the U.S. in 1986, by the early 1990s many of them had closed; Ramírez Berg, *Cinema of Solitude, A Critical Study of Mexican Film, 1967-1983*, 214.

40. Academy Visual History with Edward James Olmos, interviewed by Lourdes Portillo in Encino, May 15, 2014.

41. This mural was recently restored; see Hailey Branson-Potts, "Downtown's 'Pope of Broadway' Mural Featuring Actor Anthony Quinn Fully Restored by Original Artist," *Los Angeles Times*, January 24, 2017, http://www.latimes.com/local/lanow/la-me-ln-pope-broadway-anthony-quinn-20170124-story.html. The depiction of Hollywood actors in Torres' mural art is chronicled in the documentary *Eloy Take Two* (Roberto S. Oregel, 2009).

42. See David R. Maciel and María Rosa García-Acevedo, "The Celluloid Immigrant," in *Culture Across Borders: Mexican Immigration and Popular Culture* (Tucson, AR: University of Arizona Press, 1998), 174.

43. Lawrence Cohn, "'Like Water' Crossover A Spanish-Lingo Record," *Variety*, June 21, 1993, 7, *Como agua para chocolate* Production and Clippings Files, Margaret Herrick Library, Academy of Motion Picture Arts and Sciences, Los Angeles, California.

44. See Harry P. Pachón, Louis DeSipio, Rodolfo O. de la Garza, and Chon A. Noriega, "Missing in Action: Latinos in and out of Hollywood," in *The Future of Latino Independent Media: A NALIP Sourcebook*, ed. Chon A. Noriega (Los Angeles: UCLA Chicano Studies Research Center, 2000), 19, 24–25.

45. Nielsen Company, "Popcorn People: Profiles of the U.S. Moviegoer Audience," January 2013, cited in Idelisse Malavé and Esti Giordani, *Latino Stats: American Hispanics by the Numbers* (New York: The New Press, 2015), 107.

46. Mary Beltrán, *Latina/o Stars in U.S. Eyes* (Urbana: University of Illinois Press, 2009), 111.

47. See Gary M. Stern, "Why the Dearth of Latino Directors?" *Cineaste* 19, nos. 2–3 (1992): 45; for research data on Latinx careers in Hollywood, including SAG members, see Pachón, DeSipio, et. al. "Missing in Action: Latinos In and Out of Hollywood," 15–58.

48. Interestingly, Zuzana M. Pick's book on the subject concludes its discussion with cinema produced in exile by Marilú Mallet, Fernando Solanas, and Raúl Ruiz; see Pick, *The New Latin American Cinema: A Continental Project* (Austin, TX: University of Texas Press, 1993), 157–185.

49. Helena Solberg-Ladd, "The View from the United States," in Julianne Burton, *Cinema and Social Change in Latin America: Conversations with Filmmakers* (Austin, TX: University of Texas Press, 1986), 101.

50. For a definition of this term, and its application to Chicanx cinema, see Rosa-Linda Fregoso, *The Bronze Screen: Chicana and Chicano Film Culture*, 52–54.

51. Academy Visual History with Arturo Ripstein, interviewed by Lourdes Portillo in Mexico City, September 23, 2015.

FILM FESTIVALS
PUNTOS DE ENCUENTRO/
POINTS OF ENCOUTER

BY: LAURA ISABEL SERNA

Multiple Academy Award winner and giant of both Mexican cinema and Hollywood, Alejandro González Iñárritu recalls the unusual path his first feature film *Amores perros* (2000) took on its way to international critical acclaim. With a limited sense of how festival submissions work, he decided to send the film, composed of three interlocking stories, to the Cannes Film Festival. There, the curator of Latin American films rejected the film as too violent, too long, and generally inappropriate for submission to the festival's main competition. "Back then and for over 40 years," Iñárritu remembers, "besides some films from Buñuel, Emilio Fernandez, and Ripstein, it was almost impossible for a Mexican film to get into Cannes."[1]

After contemplating sending the film directly to the committee, he and his producers decided to send it to Critics' Week, a festival side bar that features first or second films that screen Out of Competition. The buzz the film created when it screened, becoming "the film you have to see," took Iñárritu by surprise. He had never been to a festival, much less Cannes; perhaps people were just being polite.

In his Academy Visual History Interview, conducted as part of the Academy's *Pacific Standard Time: LA/LA* project, he tells the story of the jury's outrage—the best film of the festival was screening Out of Competition—and how this underdog film, no pun intended, got widespread distribution out of the controversy and critical attention. "It won the attention that it needed, and it became sort of an underdog story," he recounts, "and that was a beautiful experience. It helped open the door again to wonderful Mexican and Latin American films that have been selected and winning awards in Cannes for the last 15 years."[2]

Though it is true that more Latin American films than ever have found their way into the festival's

official competition, this has not been the case every year. While in 2000 there was only one Latin American film in competition, in 2008 there were three. Latin American films also appear regularly as part of *Un Certain Regard*, which recognizes first films, or in the festivals' Out of Competition screenings.[3]

Iñárritu's tale of *Amores perros*' almost accidental success at Cannes illustrates the power of festivals in shaping the fortunes of Latin American directors and their films. Festivals clearly create opportunities—*Amores perros*, which went on to earn Mexico an Academy Award nomination for Foreign Language Film, is a case in point. But, festivals also serve as gatekeepers of film culture, deciding which films have

the opportunity to be screened and sometimes even, which films will ultimately get made. Indeed, festivals have a strong hand in shaping categories such as "Latin American cinema." More so because festivals are frequently curated according to regions, Asia, Latin America, etc., and films and filmmakers are discussed with reference to their country of origin.

Elaborating how the category of Latin American Cinema has been defined in the context of the global film circuit is beyond the scope of this modest essay. Briefly, however, festivals determine what constitutes a "quality" film, with the implication that quality should represent the filmic output of any given country on the world stage. What is more,

categories and definitions for both artists and films. To better understand the role that festivals play, the first part of this essay surveys the appearance of Latin American films at three types of festivals: marquee festivals such as Cannes, independent film festivals in the United States, and Latino film festivals in the U.S. I then shift focus to examine the crucial role that festivals have played in shaping the trajectories of specific films and directors' careers.

At the outset, it is important to distinguish between Latin American films and filmmakers and their Latino counterparts.[7] Though frequently conflated in popular discourse, for the purposes of this essay I will use Latin American to refer to films that come from other parts of the hemisphere, and Latino to indicate films made by Latin American immigrants to the United States and their children, and that deal with Latino themes or feature Latino characters. Though the trajectories of these groups are intertwined, they each have distinct histories of circulation and reception on the international film scene. Here, I focus primarily on Latin American film.

LATIN AMERICAN FILMS AT FESTIVALS: A BRIEF HISTORY

In the 1940s Latin American cinema began to make waves at international film festivals. For example, Emilio "El Indio" Fernández's *María Candelaria* won the Palme d'Or at Cannes in 1946, while Luis Buñuel, the Spanish-expatriate director living and working in Mexico, won the festival's best director award in 1951 for *Los olvidados*. In the 1960s, Buñuel

Previous Page: Still from *El Norte* (Gregory Nava, 1983).
Left: Alejandro G. Iñárritu and Gael García Bernal on the set of *Amores perros* (2000).

Right: Emilio Echevarría in *Amores perros* (Alejandro González Iñárritu, 2000).

festivals typically promote the work of directors as auteurs (the director as the dominant creative force), and reward novelty insofar as films remain more or less consistent with what constitutes a festival film. Film scholar Cindy H. Wong defines the festival film as having a serious tone, visual austerity, and an open narrative structure.[4] Though some festival films find wide commercial release, many films only circulate on the festival circuit which further reinforces the identity they have been assigned in the course of the programming process.

Scholars of film and media studies have recently turned their attention to festivals, generating accounts of the cultural and social impact of festivals

with long histories such as Cannes, and the newer festivals that have emerged around the globe such as the Toronto Film Festival and the Hong Kong International Film Festival.[5] Festivals in Latin America, and Latin American participation in what is now a global festival circuit—not to mention Latino film festivals in the United States—have received far less critical attention.[6] In this short essay, I mine the recollections of the filmmakers featured in the Academy's *Pacific Standard Time: LA/LA* project to sketch how festivals have shaped the trajectory of Latin American film. As these filmmakers observe, festivals can generate critical attention and provide filmmakers with opportunities to connect with potential funders, but they can also create limiting

again received recognition for the Mexico-Spain co-production *Viridiana* (1961) and the Brazilian *O pagador de promessas* (*Keeper of Promises*, Anselmo Duarte, 1962) won the Palme d'Or. This recognition at the most important international festival was sporadic; generally Latin American contributions to the festival programs of marquee festivals such as Venice, Cannes, and the Berlin Film Festival were overshadowed by "art cinema" from Europe and sometimes Asia. For example, since 1965 only two Latin American films, both from Brazil, have won Berlin's prestigious Golden Bear, Walter Salles' *Centro do Brasil* (*Central Station*, 1999) and José Padhila's *Tropa de Elite* (*Elite Squad*, 2008). And over the course of its history only one Latin American film, *From Afar* (2015) directed by Venezuelan Lorenzo Vigas, has won the Golden Lion at the Venice Film Festival.[8]

Despite this infrequency of recognition by international festival juries, prizes perform an important legitimating function. Luis Buñuel's *Los olvidados* offers a particularly clear example of this phenomenon. Upon its release in Mexico, *Los olvidados* had been heavily criticized for its dystopian view of modern Mexican society. After Buñuel's success at Cannes, Mexican critics reappraised the film as a masterpiece.[9] Indeed, Latin American films, particularly "art" or independent films, often reach an international audience composed of critics and cinephiles before or instead of reaching domestic audiences. Mexican cinema's early success at Cannes set the stage for the reception of a new wave of Latin American cinema in the following decades.

In the late 1960s rumblings of resistance to commercial, studio-produced cinema found their voice in what came to be called *Tercer Cine* (Third Cinema) or *Cinema Novo* (New Cinema) in Brazil and *El Nuevo Cine Latinoamericano* in other countries.[10]

Filmmakers from Argentina, Brazil, and Bolivia made films that embraced challenging formal characteristics to deliver powerful political critiques of capitalism, inequality, and the region's historically fraught relationship with the superpower to the north, the United States. Apiece with a new, revolutionary film culture that consisted of, not only films, but also published writing about films and filmmaking, film criticism, and film schools, a handful of important festivals were established in Latin America itself. The Festival Internacional de Cine de Viña del Mar, Chile (Viña del Mar International Film Festival), which was inaugurated in 1967 and the Festival Internacional del Nuevo Cine Latino (American International New Latin American Film Festival) founded in 1979 in Havana, Cuba, both sought to serve as incubators for politically engaged film production across the hemisphere.[11]

The films that came out of this movement found welcoming audiences at European festivals. For example, *Deus e o diabo na terra do sol* (*Black God, White Devil*, 1964) directed by Glauber Rocha and *Vidas secas* (*Barren Lives*, 1963) directed by Nelson Pereira dos Santos, both of which deal with poverty and power in the dry highlands of northeastern Brazil, screened in the official competition at Cannes in 1964.

They also began to find a place in American festivals focused on independent film. The New York Film Festival, founded in 1963, sometimes included Latin American films in its programming heavy with European art cinema and American Independent film. In 1976, Brazilian Cinema Novo director Nelson Pereira dos Santos's *Tenda dos milagres* screened during the festival to tepid reviews. The Telluride Film Festival, which began a decade later, programmed significant Latin American films including, in 1978, Chilean Helvio Soto's docudrama *Il pleut sur Santiago* (*It's Raining Over Santiago*, 1976), which recreates the September 11, 1973 military coup that toppled Salvador Allende. That timely film

Left: Poster for *Los olvidados* (*The Young and the Damned*, Luís Buñuel, 1950).
Center Right: Nelson Pereira dos Santos on the set of *Como era gostoso o meu Francês*

(*How Tasty Was My Little Frenchman*, 1971).
Right: Nelson Pereira dos Santos in Belgium with directors Agnes Varda, Wim Wenders and Werner Herzog, c.1975–1980.

was followed in 1980 by *Bye Bye Brazil,* a fanciful, introspective film that followed a troupe of down and out circus performers through Brazil's rapidly changing provinces by Carlos Diegues, one of the leading figures of Brazil's Cinema Novo movement.

Other emerging festivals embraced New Latin American Cinema with even more enthusiasm. The Filmex festival, which ran from 1971 to 1983 in Los Angeles and would eventually become American Cinematheque, gave West Coast cinephiles the opportunity to see a relatively broad selection of films that were influenced by New Latin American cinema. For example, in 1974 the festival mounted a revival screening of *Los olvidados* as well as two more recent Mexican films, Alejandro Jodorowsky's surrealist fantasy *La montaña sagrada* (*The Holy Mountain*, 1973), and Arturo Ripstein's dystopian family drama *El castillo de la pureza* (*The Castle of Purity*, 1972).[12] The 1975 festival counted Sergio Renan's *La tregua* (*The Truce,* 1974), an adaptation of a Mario Benedetti novel, and the first Argentine film to be nominated for the Academy Award for Best Foreign Language Film. Also screened at the 1975 festival was Ripstein's historical drama set in Colonial Mexico, *El santo oficio* (*The Holy Inquisition*, 1974) which was nominated for the Palme d'Or at Cannes the year of its release. In 1977, the Filmex festival featured an entire slate of Argentine films, and in 1978 it screened Tomás Gutiérrez Alea's *La última cena* (*The Last Supper*, 1976) about a slave revolt in 18th century Cuba.

Independent Latin American films fit well into Filmex's programming philosophy. In addition to showing the edgier fare produced by Hollywood studios, the festival sought out, "Films which [sic] stand little chance of being seen again in this country."[13] Its audiences were admitted "film buffs" with a taste

for international film. What is more, since Filmex was not organized around a competition, the festival had more space to showcase the latest films rather than merely those deemed the best.[14] Whether part of specific programming efforts such as the slate of Argentine films at Filmex or the surprises that sprang up periodically at the New York Film Festival, Latin American cinema was part of a broader fascination with foreign cinema that animated post-war cinema culture in the United States.[15]

Even ardent film buffs, however, had limited exposure to Latin American films because most festivals were so heavily weighted toward American independent films or European fare. This would begin to change with the emergence of festivals explicitly structured around Latino identity in the late 1970s and '80s. Niche festivals, some of which have received funding from the Academy of Motion Picture Arts and Sciences, proliferated in cities with significant Latino populations that included not only Mexican American but also Central American, Puerto Rican, and Cuban enclaves. These festivals created space for films directed by Latinos or which addressed aspects of the Latino experience in the United States, such as immigration, cultural assimilation, and discrimination. Frequently these films appeared alongside films from Latin America, whether new releases or revival screenings of classics. The organizers of these festivals saw films produced in Latin America, both contemporary and historical, as cultural resources that could help Latinos in the United States develop a sense of cultural pride and connection. What is more, these festivals not only made a wide range of films directed by Latinos or Latin Americans accessible to Latino communities in the United States, but also provided opportunities for Anglo audiences to immerse themselves in a transnational, hemispheric film culture.

The Los Angeles Latino International Film Festival (LALIFF), founded in 1996, exemplifies the goals of these types of festivals. LALIFF was founded by industry insiders: actor/director Edward James Olmos, distribution executive

Far Left: Poster for *Bye Bye Brasil* (Carlos Diegues, 1979).
Center Left: Poster for the *Filmex* film festival, 1975.

Right: Poster for *La ultima cena* (*The Last Supper*, Tomás Gutiérrez Alea, 1976).

Marlene Dermer, who had previously worked in Paramount's international division, and music producer George Hernandez. Olmos noted in 1997, "The purpose of the festival is to create a greater understanding of Latin American culture, while assisting the under-represented Latino filmmaker in Hollywood."[16] At LALIFF as at other Latino Film Festivals, Latin American and Latino films co-existed to create a hemispheric cinematic culture that linked the experiences of Chicanos and Latinos in the United States to their counterparts in Latin America.

Indeed, for Latino filmmakers, festivals have functioned as points of encounter that bring together the Latin American and U.S.-born Latino experience. Edward James Olmos acknowledges that growing up in Los Angeles, his own cinematic education did not include Latin American cinema. "I really got my big thrust [in terms of becoming familiar with Latin American cinema] when I created the Los Angles Latino International Film Festival, in which we would bring hundreds of films to Los Angeles and over a ten day period we would watch 'em [sic]."[17] Similarly, Luís Valdez, most well-known for the cinematic adaption of the play *Zoot Suit* (1981) and *La Bamba* (1987) a biopic about Chicano singer Ritchie Valens, notes that the international festivals he has attended have provided him opportunities to meet and interact with filmmakers from Latin America.[18]

As this overview suggests, festivals have been important to the trajectory of contemporary Latin American film. Festivals expose audiences and critics to new films and new talent, construct the public's notion of Latin American film history and its relationship to Latino cinema, and, frequently, bring filmmakers from across the hemisphere together.

The following section presents specific case studies to illustrate how festivals bring films to the attention of distributors and critics, allow filmmakers to secure funding, and foster independent film production across the hemisphere.

PROMOTING LATIN AMERICAN AND LATINO VOICES

Major international and independent festivals included Latin American, and somewhat less frequently, Latino films in their programming—but one organization, the Sundance Institute—developed programs in the 1990s specifically designed to encourage Latin American and Latino voices. Though they have taken various forms over the course of its history, the Institute's core programs have consisted of workshops for screenwriters and filmmakers (e.g. directors), as well as special screenings designed to nurture audiences taste for independent fare. The Institute made concerted efforts to create links with filmmakers and film industries outside of the United States, by including Latin American and Latino directors and writers in the Institute's annual labs, and collaborating with film-related institutions in Latin America to export the lab model abroad.

From its inception, the Institute's summer lab included Latino and Latin American directors and writers as both advisors and participants. Importantly, Gregory Nava's influential film *El Norte* (1983) was workshopped at the Institute's

inaugural summer lab and became the first lab film to be produced. Actor and director Edward James Olmos served as an advisor to the summer lab in its second year (1982). Beyond including U.S. Latino talent, the Institute sought to build bridges with Latin American directors and screenwriters. In 1989, the Institute hosted a writing workshop led by novelist Gabriel García Márquez, which brought seven Hispanic and one Brazilian writer together to participate in a weeklong workshop.[19]

It was this effort that attracted the attention of the young director Patricia Cardoso, who had come from Colombia to the United States on a Fulbright to study filmmaking at UCLA in the 1980s. Though she was unsuccessful in securing a spot in the workshop with Márquez, she was impressed, and started working for Sundance: "It was the first time that I saw an organization in the United States that had a program for Latin American cinema." Initially she did whatever needed to be done—stuffing envelopes, translating, etc.—until the Institute was awarded a grant from the Rockefeller Foundation to support a Latin American program.[20] That program would take the Institute's lab model to Mexico, Brazil, Chile, and even Cuba as cinema institutions and organizations across the hemisphere, such as Telefilm Canada, the Havana-based Foundation for New Latin American Cinema, and RioFilme (Brazil) collaborated with Sundance to host screenwriters workshops.

Indeed, the trade press eagerly followed the Institute's activities across the hemisphere, especially as the program gathered steam in the 1990s. As Leonard Klady describes in a 1996 article published in *Variety,* "The Latin American program began by bringing filmmakers to the existing labs. The response grew rapidly and resource people were sent to support

Sundance-style programs established in Mexico and Chile."[21] In 1993 the Institute put on a producers' workshop in Toluca, Mexico, followed in 1995 by a writers lab in Cuernavaca, Mexico in collaboration with the Instituto Mexicano de Cinematografía (IMCINE), the Universidad Nacional Autónoma de México (UNAM), and the Universidad de Guadalajara. This lab brought together participants from Mexico, Uruguay, and Argentina to work with advisors from Brazil, Argentina, Mexico, Spain, Hungary, and the United States.[22]

The Institute also sought to provide filmmakers with tools that would help them get their films produced and support film production in Latin America. Director Michelle Satter described the Institute's programming goals as "enhancing their [Latin American filmmakers'] economic resourcefulness . . . [and] supporting the next generation of talent."[23] In this way, she declared, "We [Sundance] can be a catalyst for that cinema in the world." To that end screenwriting workshops were followed by production, distribution and marketing symposia, and a producers' conference that was held in Havana in collaboration with Telefilm Canada and the Cuban International Film School. The Institute was careful, given the political situation between the United States and Cuba to emphasize that the goal of the event was to explore "ways to make Latin cinema more viable in the global marketplace."[24]

Programming like that undertaken by the Sundance Institute with support from the MacArthur and Rockefeller Foundations in the 1990s established a model that could be replicated. Latino film festivals such as the Los Angeles Latino International Film Festival and the Miami Film Festival, developed similar, if smaller programs for nurturing the talent of young screenwriters, and

exposing filmmakers and their work to producers.[25] As Patricia Cardoso notes, "When I started working [at] Proimágenes [a non-profit film organization in Colombia] . . . three or four years ago, I found out about tons of script labs all over Latin America. Sundance was the first script lab. People took that model from Sundance . . . and then people started doing it." She told Michelle Satter, [to] "look at the effect this had, it was over twenty years ago and look at the impact it has today."[26] As Cardoso observes, the Sundance Institute's programming has had a significant influence on the resurgence of filmmaking across the hemisphere.

Beyond these targeted development programs, festivals have served an important function for Latin American and Latino films that might not immediately catch the eye of commercial distributors. Film studies scholar Cindy Wong writes, "For smaller films, new directors, or less popular genres (documentary or shorts) . . . festival recognition may sustain and even create films and careers."[27] The trajectory of the 1983 film *El Norte* illustrates the role that festivals play in cultivating excitement about specific films. *El Norte* brought the struggles of Latin American migrants to the screen in vivid strokes. The film focuses on a Guatemalan brother and sister who flee political violence in their home country only to be met with discrimination in the United States. Critics heralded the film as both important and timely. Writing in the *New York Times*, Vincent Canby called it "one of the most boldly original and satirical social-political statements ever to be found in a film about the

Left: Edward James Olmos and Marlene Demer at the opening night gala of the Los Angeles Latino International Film Festival (LALIFF), 2013.

United States as a land of power as well as opportunity."[28] Janet Maslin, another *New York Times* critic described the film as a "remarkable accomplishment" and "real and involving." She singled out Nava's treatment of the film's protagonists, played by Mexican stage actors David Villalpando and Zaide Silvia Gutiérrez, whose characters guided the film's trajectory. In the early 1980s, a film told from the perspective of undocumented migrants was a revelation. Originally conceived of as a made-for-television feature, its journey to commercial distribution and eventually into the canon of both Latino and Independent American film included important stops on the festival circuit.

Nava, as many reviews noted, studied film at UCLA in the 1970s. There he completed a short film *The Journal of Diego Rodriguez Silva* (1972), which won the 1972 National Student Film Festival Drama Award, in his words, "the biggest award that any [student] film could win."[30] Nava's thesis film, *The Confessions of Amans* was a historical drama shot on 16 mm film in Spain on a budget of $20,000, part of which came from the American Film Institute. To gain exposure for the film he sought out festivals that might want to screen it. He recalls the tedious work in the days before the internet of researching festivals and reaching out to them via mail. A programmer at the Chicago Film Festival took an interest in the film. The festival organizers had prepared Nava for the fact that a 16 mm student thesis film would be of little interest to the critics attending the festival. But Roger Ebert, the one critic who did see it, called it "an astonishing achievement." Ebert highlighted that despite the film's shoestring budget of $20,000, "it plays strongly and looks great."[31] Not withstanding a lack of interest on the part of most other critics, *The Confessions* won the festival's Silver Hugo award for best new feature film.

This recognition of his first film surely helped draw the work of Nava and his then-partner Anna Thomas to the attention of the organizers of the newly formed Sundance Institute. Nava's script for *El Norte* was among the projects selected for the inaugural Institute lab in 1981. Once produced, *El Norte* premiered at Telluride. Although the film had been originally produced for public television—half of its funding came from PBS's American Playhouse series—the reaction it received at Telluride led to a commercial distribution deal. Speaking about the film's securing distribution after screening there, festival manager Stella Pence declared, "our secret love is finding those good films and getting them out there."[32] Nava remembers that screening in Telluride vividly, ". . . the reaction to that movie was unbelievable. Off the charts. I mean standing ovation, people went crazy . . . I left the theater and the staircase was crowded with people. All wanting to touch me. To take my photograph and have my photograph taken with them."[33]

El Norte continues to be a touchstone both for Latino film in the United States and American Independent cinema. In 1995, it was selected for inclusion in the National Film Registry at the Library of Congress, which highlights the most culturally significant films produced in the United States from the silent period to today. In 1999, it was re-released by Artisan Entertainment after screening at a retrospective at Sundance.[34] It continues to be shown regularly at festivals, is taught in college classrooms across the country, and was released on DVD and Blu-ray by the prestigious Criterion Collection. Indeed, descriptions of the Sundance Institute consistently point to *El Norte* as a film that "benefited from the four-week program in which aspiring directors work closely with mentors."[35] That is, the film is held up as an independent Latino production that

gained crucial exposure in the context of American independent festivals. *El Norte* functioned as a gateway film of sorts by bringing narratives that concerned the lives of not only undocumented migrants but also Latinos more broadly into the mainstream of American Independent cinema.

In addition, festivals have become one mechanism by which independent filmmakers from Latin American countries received the financial support that allows them to embark on, or finish projects. Formal or informal opportunities to network with producers and distributors and competitions with financial awards have become especially important in light of decreased state support for film production in Latin America.[36] For example Patricia Cardoso's short *Cartas al niño Dios* (*Letters to Child God*, 1991), a playful film about Christmas customs in Colombia told from the point of view of an adult remembering their childhood, was as Cardoso remembers it "in something like fifty festivals across the world and won around twenty prizes."[37] One of those prizes came with the equivalent of $20,000 dollars, money that she used to begin production on *El reino de los cielos* (*The Kingdom of Heaven*, 1994). Prize money from other festivals and competitions, such as the Herbert Bals Fund and a prize competition at the Toronto Film Festival underwritten by the MacArthur Foundation went toward postproduction. That film, like *Cartas al niño Dios,* "went to many festivals and won many prizes." Finally, her thesis film, *The Water Carrier of Cucunuba* (1994) won the Student Academy Award.

The latter award proved to be a turning point in Cardoso's career. As she remembers, "lots of people began to call me, producers . . . it screened at the Telluride Film Festival, which is a very prestigious film festival . . . a producer had seen it at Telluride and

called me."[39] That phone call resulted in her signing on to direct the dramatic-comedy *Real Women Have Curves* (2002). *Real Women* premiered at Sundance where it won the Audience Award for best dramatic film and a Special Jury Prize. As her other films had, this remarkable story that places the experience of two Latinas front and center screened at numerous other festivals and reaped a raft of awards.

Similarly, Argentine filmmaker Lucrecia Martel had made a handful of documentaries and a short,

Rey muerto (1995), which won the Coral Best Short Award at the Havana Film Festival. Her first feature film, *La ciénaga* (*The Swamp*, 2001), brought her to the attention of international audiences after exposure on the festival circuit. Her script for *La ciénaga* won the NHK Filmmakers Award for international cinema at Sundance in 1999. The award, sponsored by the Japanese public television broadcaster, includes a $10,000 prize. As one journalist noted, "she used the prize as seed money for the production."[40] Once completed, the film screened at the Berlin Film

Left: Ingrid Oliu, Lupe Ontiveros, Patricia Cardoso, America Ferrera, and Josefina López at the Sundance Film Festival premiere of *Real Women Have Curves* in 2002.

Right: Director Lucrecia Martel displays her Alfred Bauer award for *La ciénaga* (*The Swamp*), at the Berlin Film Festival in 2001.

Festival—where it won the Alfred Bauer Prize—and the Edinburgh, Telluride, Toronto, New York, Mill Valley, Chicago and Vancouver Film Festivals.

Finally, festivals can improve a film's chances of being seen in its home country, just as Cannes did for *Los olvidados* in the 1950s. Mexican director María Novaro sees the ways that international film festivals can help, as she says, "widen its [a film's] audience in Mexico . . . it helps you a lot to do well outside the country so that in Mexico they . . . pay attention to you."[41] She experienced this phenomenon, she recalls, with both *Danzón* (1991) and *Las buenas hierbas* (*The Good Herbs,* 2010). *Danzón* premiered at Cannes—it was accepted while still in postproduction—and was screened commercially in France, then made the rounds of the festival circuit. Elissa Rashkin observes that "after its premiere during the newly inaugurated Hoy en el Cine Mexicano cycle, *Danzón* went on to do what few "quality" films had done in [Mexico] in recent memory, make a profit at the box office."[42]

As these examples and the trajectory of *Amores perros* demonstrate, festivals serve an important function in generating critical attention and even funding for independent films from Latin America. Directors whose work is recognized have gone on to make commercial features or, in the case of Martel, to connect with funding to be able to continue successful independent careers. At the same time, festivals which collapse the diversity of cinematic production in a region into neat categories, can be experienced as limiting. María Novaro—and this

may stem from the fact that she has been successful—feels that her early career "was about feeling important, feeling acknowledged, traveling around

the world, I would give too much importance to festivals."[43] Lucrecia Martel, for her part, acknowledges how important festivals are in connecting films made "outside the big industry," films that go against "the model for narrative in commercial North American film," with distributors.[44] At the same time, she recognizes that festival audiences represent a very small slice of the public: "And so, the first reaction I always get to know is the audience's, the particular audience of the New York festival, which is people, in general, of a high level of education and of a high level of comfort . . . an audience that is very upper-middle class let's say . . . the rounds the films have done have always been in places where that public goes . . . that same public."[45]

Indeed, some filmmakers actively resist the tendency for festival culture to categorize both films and filmmakers. Cardoso remembers that during her time at the Sundance Institute, Arturo Ripstein had been invited to the festival but did not accept "because he refused to be identified as Latin-American . . . he was a world-famous director, he wasn't a Latin American director."[46] Ripstein himself, in the course of participating in his Academy Visual History Interview offers a pointed critique of the demands placed on non-commercial film: "We are forced to make something very strange that they call the festival film, a weird and unappetizing genre that is a cinema that only exists to go to festivals and have a certain amount of success [there] . . . Festivals accept you and they direct you, then you also enter a slimy, swampy land in which there is no precision in respect to what it's for, where it's going, and what it means."[47] In this way, Ripstein resists aligning his work to the demands of festival culture.

CONCLUSION

As recently as 2014, an MPAA survey found that Latinos who make up 17% of the U.S. population buy 23% of tickets sold to theatrical screenings.[48] In recent years more Latin American films have made it to the big screen in the United States through the efforts of distributors anxious to capitalize on this lucrative market. Companies like the distributor-producer Pantelion, a joint venture of Lionsgate Films and Mexican media powerhouse Televisa, have produced or acquired distribution rights to films that they believe will appeal to Latino audiences in the United States. One of their notable successes has been the film *No se aceptan devoluciones* (*Instructions Not Included*, Eugenio Derbez, 2013) which earned almost $45,000,000 over a sixteen-week run in the U.S., making it the fourth top-grossing foreign film of all time.[49] Other Latin American and Latino filmmakers have gone the route of independent distribution or distribution via on-line streaming services. Despite these developments, the festival circuit remains key to introducing diverse publics internationally and domestically to Latin American film. Specialized programs like those administered by Sundance in the 1990s with foundation support may not exist, but festivals have proven their importance in promoting Latin American and Latino film over the course of the last four decades. Festivals have provided opportunities for international audiences to discover the variety of films being made in Latin America, as exemplified by the tremendous impact of *Amores perros* at the Cannes Film Festival in 2000. The tremendous influence of contemporary Latin American cinema on global film culture comes in part from its success on the international festival circuit. Festivals provide venues for the exhibition of Latin American and Latino independent cinema that typically struggles to find wide distribution, bringing new films and directors to the attention of both critics and audiences. What is more, festivals connect filmmakers to the funding for independent projects, distribution, and, sometimes, opportunities to make commercial films underwritten by large studios. Though festivals can be critiqued for the ways they limit our understanding of national and regional cinema, they remain a central point of encounter between Latin American and Latino cinema and global film culture.

DR. LAURA ISABEL SERNA
Associate Professor of Cinema and Media Studies,
USC School of Cinematic Arts

Dr. Serna is the author of *Making Cinelandia: American Films and Mexican Film Culture* (Duke University Press, 2014). She has published essays on a range of topics in Mexican film culture during the silent era in journals such as *Aztlán: A Journal of Chicano Studies* and *Film History*. Her research has been supported by numerous grants and fellowships including a prestigious Andrew W. Mellon Postdoctoral Fellowship and two Fulbright-García Robles Fellowships. She is currently working on a monograph, tentatively titled *On the Latest Steamship: Silent Film Distribution in the Spanish-Speaking Caribbean*, which examines the social and commercial networks that facilitated the importation and exhibition of foreign films in the Caribbean during the teens and on a series of essays on sponsored films about, by, and for Mexican-Americans from the 1960s and '70s. She received her Ph.D. from Harvard University.

Left: Poster for *Amores perros*
(Alejandro G. Iñárritu, 2000).

NOTES

1. Academy Visual History with Alejandro G. Iñárritu, interviewed by Lourdes Portillo in Hollywood, September 2, 2016.

2. Ibid.

3. It is important to qualify this image of success. In 2016, there were no Latin American films at Cannes in any of the official programs. The only Latin American films at the festival were to be found in screenings of student work.

4. Cindy H. Wong, *Film Festivals: Culture, People, and Power on the Global Screen* (Rutgers, NJ: Rutgers University Press, 2011), 68.

5. See, for example, Marijke de Valck, Brendan Kredell, and Skadi Loist, eds. *Film Festivals: History, Theory, Practice*, (New York, NY: Routledge, 2016); Cindy H. Wong, *Film Festivals*; Richard Porton, ed. *Dekalog 3: On Film Festivals* (London: Wallflower Press, 2009); Marijke de Valck, *Film Festivals: From European Geopolitics to Global Cinephilia* (Amsterdam: Amsterdam University Press, 2007); and the chapter on Cannes in Vanessa Schwartz, *It's So French: Hollywood, Paris, and the Making of Global Film Culture* (Chicago, IL: University of Chicago Press, 2007).

6. A recent dissertation addresses the formation of the category "Latin American Cinema" from a sociological perspective: Laura Rodríguez Isaza, "Branding Latin America: Film Festivals and the International Circulation of Latin American Films," Ph.D. Dissertation, University of Leeds: School of Modern Languages and Cultures, Centre for World Cinemas, 2012. See also Luisela Alvaray, who situates festivals and film markets alongside co-production practices, regional networks, and policy measures in "National, Regional, and Global: New Waves of Latin American Cinema," *Cinema Journal* 47, no. 3 (Spring 2008): 59–60.

7. For ease of reading I use the masculine singular, which technically encompasses both genders.

8. Latino films, if not simply absent from these spaces altogether, are typically screened Out of Competition as part of thematic sidebars or other special programs that do not garner the same amount of press attention or prestige.

9. On the perception of *Los olvidados* before and after Cannes see Tomás Pérez Turrent, "Luis Buñuel in Mexico," in *Mexican Cinema*, ed. Paulo Antonio Paranaguá, trans. Ana M. López (London/Mexico City: British Film Institue, IMCINE, and Consejo Nacional Para la Cultura y las Artes de México), 203.

10. The manifesto that gave this movement its name, "Hacia un Tercer Cine" ("Toward a Third Cinema") by Fernando Solanas and Octavio Getino can be found translated into English in *New Latin American Cinema, Volume 1*, ed. Michael Martin(Detroit: Wayne State Press, 2001), 33–58. This volume also contains a number of other important statements and essays related to this film movement.

11. Ana M. López provides an excellent overview of the New Latin American Cinema in historical context in "An 'Other' History: The New Latin American Cinema," *Radical History Review* 41 (1988): 93–116.

12. Mary Murphy, FILMEX as Establishment: Survival No Longer the Problem, *Los Angeles Times*, March 21, 1976 t1.

13. Ibid.

14. Lee Grant, "Behind the Scenes with FILMEX's Guru," *Los Angeles Times* April 2, 1981, I1.

15. On the surge in foreign films in the United States after World War II see Tino Balio, *The Foreign Film Renaissance on American Screens, 1946–1973* (Madison, WI: University of Wisconsin Press, 2010).

16. Latino Film Festival Runs October 2–11, *Hollywood Reporter*, August 31, 1998, 7.

17. Academy Visual History with Edward James Olmos, interviewed by Lourdes Portillo in Encino, May 15, 2014.

18. Academy Visual History with Luís Valdez, interviewed by Lourdes Portillo in San Juan Bautista, June 8, 2014.

19. Sundance Latino Workshop Concludes, *Variety*, August 17, 1989.

20. Academy Visual History with Patricia Cardoso, interviewed by Lourdes Portillo in Hollywood, April 14, 2015.

21. Leonard Klady, "Clarion Call for Indies," *Variety*, January 17, 1996.

22. Ibid.

23. Daniel S. Moore, "Sundance Ever Warm to Latin American Fare," *Variety*, March 25–31,1996, 59.

24. Monica Roman and Rex Weiner, "U.S. Int'l Exex Flock to Cuba Cinema Confab," *Variety*, June 5, 1996.

25. LALIFF sponsored workshops for young writers, seminars, and industry luncheons. See for example, Bob Strauss, "Latino Film Fest an International Blend," *The Daily News of Los Angeles*, October 4, 2006, U6. On the Miami Film Festival's small cinema market, Encuentros, see Michael W. Sasser, "No Time to Look Back," *Sun Post*, "January 22, 2004" and Mary Sutter, "Miami Fest Tries to Boost Market," *Variety*, (February 21, 2005.

26. Academy Visual History with Patricia Cardoso, interviewed by Lourdes Portillo in Hollywood, April 14, 2015.

27. Cindy Hing-Yuk Wong, *Film Festivals*, 7.

28. Vincent Canby, "El Norte: A Fine Movie Fueled by Injustice," *New York Times* January 24, 1984, Sect. 2, 17.

29. Janet Maslin, "'El Norte' Promised Land for Guatemalans, *New York Times*, January 11, 1984.

30. Academy Visual History with Gregory Nava, interviewed by Lourdes Portillo in Beverly Hills, June 16, 2015.

31. Roger Ebert, "Festival Report," *American Film* April 1977, 53.

32. M.S. Mason, "Old Mining Town Screens Some Film Nuggets," *The Christian Science Monitor*, October 15, 1985, 33.

33. Academy Visual History with Gregory Nava, interviewed by Lourdes Portillo in Beverly Hills, June 16, 2015.

34. "Homecoming for Nava as 'El Norte' starts new trek," *Hollywood Reporter*, January 25, 1999, "El Norte Returns: Artisan Picks Up Domestic Rights to Re-Release," *Variety*, January 24, 1999.

35. See, for example, John Brodie, "Sundance Selects Film Lab Participants," *Variety*, April 26, 1994) and Caryn James,

"Pursuing Art and Angst at Bob's Movie Camp," *New York Times*, July 19, 1992.

36. This phenomenon has been widely noted. For a brief summary see Alvaray, "National, Regional, and Global," 49–50.

37. Academy Visual History with Patricia Cardoso, interviewed by Lourdes Portillo in Hollywood, April 14, 2015.

38. Ibid.

39. Ibid.

40. Leslie Camhi, "Lucrecia Martel's Domestic Disturbances: Into the Swamp," *Village Voice*, October 23, 2001.

41. Academy Visual History with María Novaro, interviewed by Lourdes Portillo in Mexico City, September 25, 2015.

42. Elissa Rashkin, *Women Filmmakers in Mexico: The Country of Which We Dream* (Austin, TX: University of Texas Press, 2001), 167.

43. Academy Visual History with María Novaro, interviewed by Lourdes Portillo in Mexico City, September 25, 2015.

44. Academy Visual History with Lucrecia Martel, interviewed by Lourdes Portillo in Hollywood, October 3, 2014.

45. Ibid.

46. Academy Visual History with Patricia Cardoso, interviewed by Lourdes Portillo in Hollywood, April 14, 2015.

47. Academy Visual History with Arturo Ripstein, interviewed by Lourdes Portillo in Mexico City, September 23, 2015.

48. Motion Picture Association of America (MPAA), "Theatrical Market Statistics 2014," Sherman Oaks, CA: MPAA, 2015.

49. See figures at Box Office Mojo: http://www.boxofficemojo.com/movies/?page=main&id=instructionsnotincluded.htm, accessed January 2, 2017.

HOW LATIN AMERICA BECAME AN OVERLOOKED EPICENTER OF INTERNATIONAL CINEMA

BY CARLOS A. GUTIÉRREZ

The first two decades of the new century have witnessed a significant cinematic renaissance in Latin America. Without bells and whistles, dogmas, or manifestos, and largely influenced and inspired by the experience of the so-called New Argentinean Cinema, a young and enthusiastic generation of filmmakers has been drastically changing how Latin America sees and represents itself on the big screen.

This renaissance has gone hand in hand with the region's major political shifts,[1] produced an impressive body of artistic work, and launched the professional careers of many filmmakers, who—through their approach—are challenging traditional notions of politics, culture, and identity. Formerly taboo topics such as race relations, religion, the military, and gender, have been explored by younger generations of filmmakers from both the art-house and mainstream cinema, with record box office numbers indicating public enthusiasm.

On the strength of all that has been happening—the increased production, diversified filmmaking, and unparalleled recognition on the international level—an opportunity has presented itself to question the general notion of Latin American cinema as a singular entity. Although filmmakers in the region are producing work that goes well beyond old tropes of national and regional identity, too often the collective body of work continues to be pigeonholed by the reigning Eurocentrism of international film programming and criticism pertaining to a mostly homogenous population. The art house, though an important support for these films in the U.S., continues with its structures of celebrating exoticism and otherness, to deny the existence of the many dialogues occurring within Latin American cinema. As these younger Latin American filmmakers have used globalization to their advantage, there is even

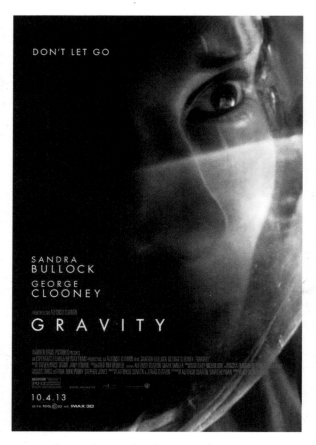

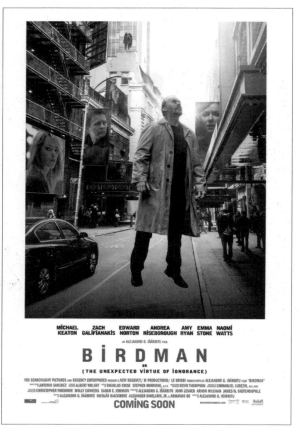

more of a need to probe the idea of Latin American as plural, heterogeneous cinemas.

The case for such a reconsideration of Latin American cinemas would be harder to make were it not for the notable achievements of these films and filmmakers in multiple arenas, namely: Hollywood, the international film festival circuit, the home-country box offices, and local production. In imagining how to begin thinking of Latin American cinema in terms of multiple cinemas, it is

helpful to look at the New Argentinean Cinema that cleared the way for the past two decades of growth, as well as to examine the early successes of several of the region's leading filmmakers who benefited from that break with past traditional cinematic themes, and created works that have had an international impact and influenced the broadening of cinema in the region that continues to the present.

These topics are addressed in depth below, but before doing so, it is worth looking at some of the recent acclaim earned by several notable Latin American filmmakers who are emblematic of this renaissance. Not that long ago, it would have been unthinkable that a Mexican director would win an Academy Award for Best Director. So, it's astonishing that Mexican filmmakers Alfonso Cuarón and Alejandro G. Iñárritu achieved the feat of winning that very prize three years in a row: Cuarón for *Gravity* in 2014, and Iñárritu in 2015 for *Birdman* and again in 2016 for *The Revenant*.

The recognition has not only been in Hollywood; numerous festival prizes have been awarded to Latin American films in recent years. Two Mexican directors won the Best Director Award at the Cannes Film Festival—arguably the most influential film festival in the world—back-to-back in 2012 and 2013: Carlos Reygadas for *Post Tenebras Lux* (2012), and, a year later, Amat Escalante for *Heli*. Jayro Bustamante's debut feature *Ixcanul* won the Silver Bear Alfred Bauer Prize at the 2015 Berlinale, marking the highest award ever won by a Central American film production.

The success of these films can also be measured by the drastic increase in film production; in the past decade, many Latin American countries saw record-breaking numbers of films made. For example, Costa Rica, the Central American country of only 4.8 million inhabitants produced roughly twenty feature films since 1930, but almost duplicated that amount between 2014 and 2015.

Mexico has become the fourth-largest film-exhibition market in the world after China, India, and the United States, and more local audiences are flocking to see national films. The country broke all-time production records in 2015 with 140 feature films, and again in 2016 with 162 films, more than at

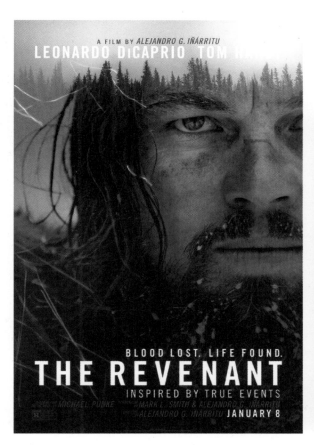

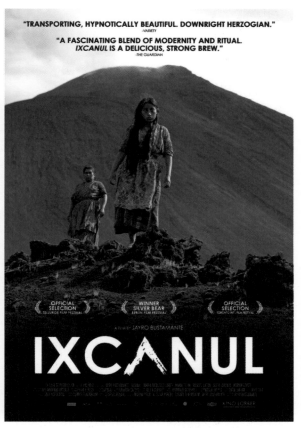

the height of the so-called Golden Age of Mexican cinema of the 1940s and early 1950s.[2]

Brazil saw the theatrical release of 139 local films in 2016, including the Biblical epic, *Os Dez Mandamentos* (*The Ten Commandments*) by Alexandre Avancini (based on the TV series of the same name), which was released in the summer of 2016 and broke the all-time attendance record with over 14 million viewers in its theatrical run. Box office records have been broken in Argentina,[3] Costa Rica,[4]

Colombia,[5] Peru, Uruguay, Venezuela, and other countries in Latin America.[6]

But from where did all this talent and influence originate? Why, despite its influence and accolades,

Previous Page: Still from *Centro do Brasil* (*Central Station*, Walter Salles, 1998) Far Left: Poster for *Gravity* (Alfonso Cuarón, 2013). Center Left: Poster for *Birdman*

(Alejandro G. Iñárritu, 2014). Center Right: Poster for *The Revenant* (Alejandro G. Iñárritu, 2015). Right: Poster for *Ixcanul* (Jayro Bustamante, 2016).

does Latin American cinema and its filmmakers remain, for the most part, overlooked by the international gate-keepers of mainstream and art-house cinemas? And, after almost two decades of continuous production, what are the challenges ahead for film production as many Latin American countries undergo significant political changes, and the 2016 U.S. presidential election portends an era of uncertain international geopolitics?

NEW ARGENTINEAN CINEMA

The 1980s were, for the most part, a brutal time for Latin America. Dictatorship and authoritarian regimes, civil wars, and perennial economic crises characterized the region during this period, which in many countries was labeled as the "lost decade." Film-wise, it was very much the same case. Despite a few specific examples, Latin American cinema suffered a major crisis and film production took a deep plunge for several years.

A shift occurred in the late 1990s. A young group of loosely affiliated filmmakers,[7] in a very modest way, decided to turn away from the highly allegorical and heavily political cinema of the preceding generation with low-budget productions containing more minimal narratives and an international scope, breaking with the hegemonic notions of national cinema.

Largely influenced by Martín Rejtman—whose 1992 film *Rapado* (The Cropped Head) became a cult film of sorts that discreetly paved the way toward an independent mode of production—and propelled by a new groundbreaking cinema law in 1994

UN CERTAIN REGARD
OFFICIAL SELECTION CANNES 2001

4L / musaluppi / rejtman / trapero

la libertad

una película de -a film by- lisandro alonso

that created a state production fund from revenue derived from a tax on movie tickets, a number of new filmmakers, many of them alumni of the Universidad del Cine in Buenos Aires, took the local and international scene by storm.

Israel Adrián Caetano (Uruguayan-born) and Bruno Stagnaro's slacker drama *Pizza, Beer and Cigarettes* (*Pizza, birra, faso,* 1998), officially heralded what would be christened "New Argentinean Cinema" (a recycled label used in other peak moments throughout the history of Argentine cinema). The film about a struggling group of friends who turn to robbery to make a living was novel and fresh and excited local audiences and critics alike. Shortly afterward, the international film festival took notice of Pablo Trapero's debut feature film *Crane World* (*Mundo grúa*, 1999) about a man who tries to cope with life after he loses his job. The film won the Tiger Award for Best Film at the Rotterdam Film Festival. That same year, Rejtman premiered

his sophomore production, the deadpan comedy *Silvia Prieto*.

Two years later *La ciénaga*, the celebrated and auspicious debut feature by Lucrecia Martel, had its world premiere at the Berlin Film Festival, winning the Silver Bear Alfred Bauer Prize. The film, a poignant portrait of a family divided by class and set in the northern region of Salta in Argentina, became an instant classic and established Martel as one of the most important filmmakers of her generation.[8] She followed up with *The Holy Girl* (*La niña santa*, 2004) and *The Headless Woman* (*La mujer sin cabeza*, 2008) at the official competition at the Cannes Film Festival.

Lisandro Alonso's crucial *La libertad* from 2001—which premiered at Cannes in the "Un Certain Regard" section—follows Misael Saavedra, an actual woodsman, in his daily routine. *La libertad* had, and continues to have, a major effect on filmmakers who toy with the borders of fiction and non-fiction cinema, even though it never had a theatrical release in the United States. Also premiering at Cannes was Caetano's solo directorial debut *Bolivia*, a grim drama about a Bolivian immigrant working at a restaurant in Buenos Aires, which received the Young Critics Award.

The massive Argentinean political and financial meltdown at the end of 2001 proved beneficial for the nascent film scene, as it provided creative fuel for the emerging talent. The New Argentinean

Left: Still from *La niña santa* (*The Holy Girl,* Lucrecia Martel, 2002).

Right: Publicity postcard for *La libertad* (Lisandro Alonso, 2001).

Cinema became an example that was soon imitated in other parts of South America, paving the way for talent across the region. In Argentina these past, almost two decades have created an extraordinary generation of filmmakers, including, among those not yet mentioned, Celina Murga, Mariano Llinás, the late Fabián Bielinsky, Santiago Mitre, Albertina Carri, Diego Lerman, Rodrigo Moreno, Carlos Sorín, Daniel Burman, and Damián Szifron, just to name a few.

AMORES PERROS, Y TU MAMÁ TAMBIÉN, AND CITY OF GOD

Around the same time, Alejandro González Iñárritu—whose background in Communication Studies[9] helped him build a successful career in radio and later in advertising—made his international debut with *Amores perros*, which had its world premiere at Cannes' Critics' Week in 2000, winning the top prize of the section.

The triptych drama of three distinct stories connected by a car accident in Mexico City heralded a new moment, as it was enthusiastically embraced as a different, exciting type of Mexican cinema. It premiered right after the Mexican elections of 2000, in which President Vicente Fox beat the candidate of the Mexican ruling party that had governed the country continuously for 71 years. "There was a feeling of change, a feeling that the old was over, a new century was starting, a new party was starting, and the film enters this whiff of novelty and hope, so it was a very fortunate moment" says Iñárritu.[10]

Beyond Mexico, *Amores perros* opened the door to Latin American cinema in the U.S., and Iñárritu's young and charismatic lead actor, Gael García Bernal, would provide a recognizable face for emerging Latin American cinema for years to come.

Written by Guillermo Arriaga, *Amores perros* premiered in the U.S. at the New York Film Festival and was theatrically released by Lionsgate in March 2001, earning a nomination for Best Foreign Language Film at the 73rd Academy Awards, the first for a Mexican film after a drought of twenty-five years.

In 2002, Brazil added to the international visibility of Latin American cinema with *City of God* (*Cidade de Deus*) by Fernando Meirelles, co-directed with Kátia Lund. The film, a hyperkinetic tale that takes place over the course of two decades and is set in the photogenic favelas of Rio de Janeiro, was screened Out of Competition at the Cannes Film Festival, got a successful U.S. theatrical release due to distribution by Miramax (playing in theaters for several months), and received four Academy Award nominations: Best Director, Best Cinematography, Best Editing, and Best Adapted Screenplay.

Also in 2002, Mexican director Alfonso Cuarón returned home to direct the highly popular coming-of-age film *Y tu mamá también,* starring Gael García Bernal and Diego Luna. After his 1991 debut feature *Sólo con*

tu pareja (*Love in the Time of Hysteria*) Cuarón directed a couple of Hollywood productions about which he felt ambivalent. That experience, plus the frustration of a canceled project,[11] made him look south.

Y tu mamá también was a big box office success in Mexico, and had a solid theatrical stateside release by IFC Films, earning $13.62 million, a considerable amount for a foreign-language film that was released for the art-house circuit. Even though Mexico, in a controversial decision, didn't submit the film as its Oscar candidate, *Y tu mamá también* went on to get a nomination for Best Original Screenplay at the 75th Academy Awards in 2003.

Uniquely, what Iñárritu, Meirelles, and Cuarón were able to achieve was box office success, both

locally and internationally, that merged the border between art-house and industrial cinema, seducing both Cannes and Hollywood, and creating a global cultural phenomenon.

THE BOOM IN LATIN AMERICA FILM PRODUCTION

The experience of the low-budget, yet ground-breaking productions of the New Argentinean Cinema and the emergence and success of the above-mentioned global auteurs inspired countless numbers of young, enthusiastic filmmakers throughout the region to embrace cinema as a means to drastically challenge and change Latin America traditional representations. What no one could have ever foreseen at the beginning of the new century was that this trend in Latin American cinema would be so long and influential.

Countries like Uruguay, Chile,[12] Peru,[13] and more recently Colombia,[14] have greatly contributed to the revitalization of cinema in the region, which has proved to be highly contagious. After almost two decades of increasing film production, an extensive generation of filmmakers has established itself and includes new talent from countries that historically lacked a solid film tradition, such as Panama, Guatemala, and the Dominican Republic.

Many of the filmmakers of this generation are in their thirties and early forties, although younger

Far Left: Alejandro G. Iñárritu accepting the nomination certificate awarded to Mexico for *Amores perros*, at the Academy's Foreign Language Awards celebration in 2001.

Center Left: Diego Luna, Maribel Verdú and Gael García Bernal in *Y tu mamá también* (Alfonso Cuarón, 2001).

Right: Still from *Cidade de Deus* (*City of God*, Fernando Meirelles, 2002).

ones have been joining the ranks. Moreover, some seasoned directors from previous generations have remained active—such as documentarian Patricio Guzmán from Chile, and feature directors Arturo Ripstein from Mexico, Nelson Pereira dos Santos from Brazil, and Víctor Gaviria from Colombia, to mention just a few—and in varying ways have continued contributing their experience and talent to their respective national cinemas.

One of the key elements of this revitalization has been the creation of new and creative hybrid forms of productions, which can be categorized in three distinctive forms: public support from the governments, innovative tax incentives that have allowed for the injection of private funds from corporations and companies, and fluid co-production treaties, particularly with European countries and among the Latin America countries.

The 1994 Argentinean cinema law served as an example for countries such as Brazil, Mexico, and Colombia to follow and enrich with their own experiences. Mexico, for example, launched the Fondo para la Producción Cinematográfica de Calidad (FOPROCINE) in 1998, to specifically support the film production of art-house cinema; the Fondo de Inversión y Estímulos al Cine (FIDECINE) in 2002, an innovative state film fund in the form of a loan to support commercial productions; and the Estímulo Fiscal para la Producción Cinematográfica (EFICINE 226/189) in 2006, which allow corporations to put funds into film productions as tax exemptions.

The fortunate combination of these hybrid production resources and low-budget film concepts have been fruitful enough to enable artistic freedom to live at the core of film production in Latin America, and allow filmmakers to take artistic and creative risks, even—to an extent—within mainstream cinema. Take for instance the Mexican box office record-breaking and Oscar-nominated film *The Crime of Father Amaro* (*El crimen del padre Amaro*, 2002) by Carlos Carrera, which unmasks the corruption within the Catholic Church through the story of a young priest (played by García Bernal) who falls in love with a teenage girl; or the highly popular Chilean film *Machuca* (2004) by Andrés Wood, an incisive class portrait set in 1973—the year of the infamous coup d'état—telling the story of two friends whose relationship is strained by the turbulent social and political upheaval of the era.

Additionally, we've seen the emergence of an important group of film producers that has accompanied this generation of directors, helping to protect the artistic integrity of the projects, as well as helping with the red tape involved in the application and rendering of the state and private funds, and international co-productions. Some key producers of the region include Lita Stantic and Hernán Musaluppi from Argentina; Fernando Epstein from Uruguay; Bertha Navarro, Mónica Lozano, and Pablo Cruz from Mexico; Pablo and Juan de Dios Larraín from Chile; Rodrigo Teixeira and Vania Catania from Brazil; Diana Bustamante from Colombia; and the late British producer Donald Ranvaud.

Another key element of this cinematic trend in Latin America resides in its diversity. The eclectic modes of production that developed in many of these countries have allowed different types of film themes, narratives, and aesthetics to flourish. The mainstream cinema of the local countries coexists with the independent filmmakers, recently joined by many visual artists[15] who have found in film a good opportunity to expand their artistic practices and reach new audiences. Additionally, particularly in the largest countries of the region, other cities besides the nations' capitals have become influential film capitals, as is the case of Recife in Brazil, Córdoba in Argentina, and Guadalajara in Mexico. In this sense, one could argue that in addition to talking about Latin American cinemas—in plural—it would be constructive to apply the same phrase to the larger national cinemas, thus discussing the Argentinean, the Mexican, and the Brazilian cinemas.

A third significant characteristic of this cinematic reemergence has been the defiance by its participants of traditional notions of the political. In the late 1960s and 1970s Latin America had stormed the international academic and curatorial world circuit with the militant and activist political cinema of the so-called New Latin American Cinema, fueled by the post-revolutionary Cuban cinema along with Brazil's Cinema Novo and Argentina's Documentary Film School of Santa Fe, which coined and shaped the influential notion of "Third Cinema."[16]

In the recent and ongoing generational shift that has paralleled various local political contexts, the younger Latin American directors opted for more nuanced portrayals and depictions of politics. In many instances, these representations greatly contrasted with the heavy political allegories for which the region's body of cinematic work had been celebrated.

"We don't believe in reality. We don't believe reality is already constructed, and there's nothing else to do but to accept it," says Martel.[17] And she adds, "This focus on the perception, trying to see, and trying to discover small details in reality, doesn't have to do with the expression of

a personal, intimate world, but rather with a political stand regarding reality as something that can be transformed (…) Cinema gives filmmakers and people working in film the opportunity to use the audiovisual narrative as a tool to break down perception, and that is a political action."

In contrast to past tropes of the cinema of the region, i.e. social issue concerns, chronicling the struggles of the masses, describing the rural experience, or the obsession with finding a national identity, contemporary Latin American cinema has introduced fresh concerns and preoccupations. For one, we've seen more attempts to unapologetically describe the experience of the urban middle classes, embrace the idiosyncratic, and challenge preconceived notions of Latin American-ness.

Take for example, Reygadas's *Silent Light*, a fiction film set in a Mennonite community in the state of Chihuahua in Mexico, and spoken in Plautdietsch, a German dialect; the Brazilian documentary *Santiago* by João Moreira Salles, a self-reflexive film about the director's Argentinean childhood butler as a lens for class issues in filmmaking practices; and Matías Piñeiro's series of joyous Shakespearean-related studies of young actors in Buenos Aires.

DE AQUÍ Y DE ALLÁ (FROM HERE AND THERE)

Contrary to popular belief, many of the filmmakers who have met with recent success in Latin America have either expressly decided to stay in their place of origin to develop a film career or continue to shoot mainly in their local country if they have moved abroad. For a large group of directors, the existing conditions in Latin America have

enabled them to continue filming and build a robust filmography there. In this sense, and in contrast to almost the entire rest of the world these days, many of these filmmakers in their thirties and forties have been able to direct three, four, or even more films, regardless of whether their productions ultimately secure any distribution or exhibition. This is exemplified by the fact that all five original filmmakers of the New Argentinean Cinema: Rejtman, Martel, Alonso, Trapero and Caetano decided to stay in Buenos Aires, where they have continued to expand their filmography. Only Trapero announced his plans, in 2016, to direct a couple of

English-language films: *The Man in the Rockefeller Suit* for Fox Searchlight Pictures and *Thin Skinned Animal*, for Studiocanal and independent production powerhouse Working Title.

Concurrently, and unmistakably, a group of Latin American filmmakers has thrived in Hollywood. In addition to the so-called Three Amigos (Iñárritu, Alfonso Cuarón, and Guillermo del Toro), who have

Alejandro G. Iñárritu, Guillermo del Toro, and Alfonso Cuarón arrive at the 79th Annual Academy Awards ceremony on February 25, 2007.

captured the spotlight, there is a larger group of film-makers working in the American film industry, among them the Mexican-born filmmakers Rodrigo García, Patricia Riggen, and Alfredo de Villa; Colombian-born Patricia Cardoso; Puerto Rican-born Miguel Arteta; as well as Argentinean-born Andrés Muschietti and Uruguayan-born Fede Álvarez, both of whom have contributed to revitalizing the horror genre in American mainstream cinema.

Latin American filmmakers have, for the most part, used globalization to their advantage, not only in the form of international co-productions but by redefining local and international identities. With the new technologies and shifts in geopolitical trends and culture, the potential areas of influence for a filmmaker are much greater than their city or country of residence. Filmmakers can have fluid national, and global, identities without having to cut their local ties at all.

"I never lived in Los Angeles,"[18] says Cuarón, contrary to what people might assume, adding, "The noise of the factory doesn't let me sleep at night," referring to the American film industry. After his debut feature *Sólo con tu pareja*, the London-based director made a couple of films for Hollywood studios (*A Little Princess*, 1995, and *Great Expectations*, 1998), then returned to Mexico to direct *Y tu mamá también*, earning him the reputation of an international auteur. This success got him invited to direct *Harry Potter and the Prisoner of Azkaban* (2004),[19] before making *Children of Men* (2006) and *Gravity* (2013). At the end of 2016, he returned to Mexico City to shoot his eighth feature film, *Roma*, set during the student riots of the early 1970s.[20]

There are many independent Latin American directors residing in different parts of the world,

outside of their countries of origin, such as Brazilian-born Karim Aïnouz, based in Berlin; Colombian-born Lina Rodríguez and Juan Andrés Arango, both living in Canada; Venezuelan-born Jonathan Jakubowicz, based in Los Angeles; Peruvian-born Llosa, who lives in Barcelona; and the prolific Mexican-born director Nicolás Pereda, who—after living in Canada for several years—is currently based in New York City. These filmmakers are predominantly still shooting in their countries of origin, but have also been able to tap into additional sources of funding in their places of residence.

There is also a group of U.S.-based Latin American filmmakers who are working more within the intersection of American independent cinema and foreign cinema; it includes New York-based Argentinean directors Piñeiro and Julia Solomonoff, as well as Chilean director Sebastián Silva. Coincidentally, for the first time for all three, they shot and set their most recent productions in New York City— Silva's *Nasty Baby* (2015), Piñeiro's

Left: Director Patricia Riggen with Eugenio Derbéz on set of *Miracles from Heaven* (2016).

Right: Director Claudia Llosa behind the camera on set of *La teta asustado* (*Milk of Sorrow*, 2009).

Hermia & Helena (2016), and Solomonoff's *Nobody's Watching* (*Nadie nos mira, 2017*)—the three weaving their own hybrid cultural experiences into the narratives of their films.

Then there are filmmakers like Michel Franco, who shot his English-language feature and Cannes winner, *Chronic* starring Tim Roth in Los Angeles, though he's based in Mexico City. An opposite case is director Roberto Sneider who is based in Los Angeles but makes his films in Mexico: *You're Killing Me Susana* (*Me estás matando Susana*, 2006) and his previous *Tear this Heart Out* (*Arráncame la vida*, 2008). Other Latin American filmmakers who have directed films in the Hollywood system, without having to permanently relocate to the U.S., are Brazilian director Meirelles (*The Constant Gardener*, 2005; *360*, 2011), Walter Salles (*Dark Water*, 2005; *On the Road*, 2012), José Padhila (*RoboCop*, 2014), and more recently, Chilean director Pablo Larraín (*Jackie*, 2016).

CHALLENGES, BOTH ONGOING AND NEW

For all the influence, accolades, and artistry, cinema from Latin America remains largely overlooked and underrepresented abroad. For one, the creative explosion in the region has been extremely individual and dissimilar within each nation's and region's film production. The resulting films defy simple classification—the first ingredient traditionally needed to be internationally marketed as a national auteur movement (i.e. "Iranian New Wave," "Romanian New Wave Cinema," "Korean New Wave," and so on). Except for the New Argentinean Cinema,[21] it seemed counterproductive

to try to create a unifying overarching narrative for the production of the whole region.

As stated earlier, while the international film circuit has shown recent excitement for the cinema of Latin America, the number of films from the region

programmed in their lineups remains largely limited and in many cases the validation of Latin American film production continues to revolve around some archaic and exoticizing neocolonial narrative tropes (e.g. poverty, post-apocalypse, or magical realism). It is still a common practice for Latin America to be politically or culturally reduced by film programmers (and other film professionals) to truisms of exotic ideals of a political revolution, stuck in the aftermath of the Cold War, or of post-apocalyptic underdeveloped societies where there's no rule of law. The majority of recently produced films don't fall into these stereotypes of Latin American culture, and, as previously mentioned, do not fit previous patterns of political paradigms.

Furthermore, as a direct consequence of the limited validation in the film festival circuit—and as happens with most foreign cinema in the United States—securing theatrical distribution is becoming more difficult. In these past five years, an average of roughly thirty Latin American feature films were released in U.S. theaters each year, which represents a mere five percent of the production total.

This, in turn, also hinders the films' chances at home and in Latin America. With the geopolitics of film validation still dominated by Europe and the United States, many Latin American films and directors need that external validation in order to be re-exported back to their countries of origin, just to secure distribution platforms and visibility there.

"Mexican cinema has evolved enormously. There is great talent, great films, great documentaries, and a lot of movement. But

I feel like a big challenge is that it is still difficult for people to access those movies in Mexican theatres, so in a way the distribution still needs to evolve and catch up with the talent," says Iñárritu about the challenges of current Mexican cinema.[22]

Despite more recent efforts in creating new national and regional digital distribution platforms—for example, FilminLatino and Retina Latina—the expectations of reaching larger audiences for the Latin American cinemas within the region are not very promising.

The fact that Cinema Studies as an academic endeavor remains largely Eurocentric, having a direct influence on the formation of film professionals (film critics, programmers, distributors, publicists, etc.)

leaves the cinemas of Latin American sandwiched between that obsolete binary that was what was once categorized by Latin American film theorists as "First" and "Second Cinema," the former largely represented by Hollywood, the latter embodied by the Western European art-house tradition, with the Cannes Film Festival as its pinnacle.

In the United States, where there has been an emergence of a new and influential generation of Latin American talent in Hollywood, U.S.-born Latinos, unfortunately, have lost ground within the American industry. Some Latin American filmmakers have made great strides in Hollywood, with a few conquering heroes, perhaps, but for the most part, they had to sacrifice Latino narratives for global narratives. In this sense, issues of representation and accessibility for U.S. Latinos are still timely and urgent.

The political changes of 2016, along with new financial clouds, have affected the region in countries such as Brazil and Argentina, and these shifts have the potential to influence many of the film production and financing practices that are in place and have been so helpful in the ways described.

And despite all that these two decades have meant for Latin American cinema, there's still very little critical and academic information available, with many of the filmmakers remaining largely unknown—even within the international film circuit. It will take an enormous revisionist process to fully understand this creative output and its implications, to grasp Latin American cinema in its complexity, and fully understand it beyond the traditional, outdated, and limited notions of national cinema.

CARLOS A. GUTIÉRREZ
Curator and Film Program Director,
New York, NY

Mr. Gutiérrez is co-founder and executive director of Cinema Tropical, the New York-based media arts non-profit organization that is the leading presenter of Latin American cinema in the United States. As a guest curator, he has presented several film series at different cultural institutions, including The Museum of Modern Art, the Guggenheim Museum, BAMcinématek, the Film Society of Lincoln Center, and Anthology Film Archives. He co-curated the 53rd edition of the Robert Flaherty Film Seminar, and is co-director of the Tucson Cine Mexico festival in Arizona. He is a contributing editor to BOMB magazine and has served as a member of the jury and panelist for various film festivals and funds including the Morelia Film Festival, the Margaret Mead Film Festival, SANFIC, DocsMX, the Sundance Documentary Fund, and the Tribeca Film Institute's Latin American Media Arts Fund.

Left: Poster for
The Constant Gardener
(Fernando Meirelles, 2005)

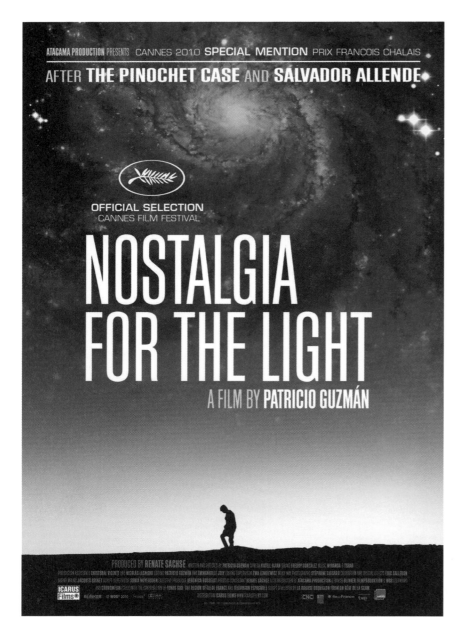

NOTES

1. Special thanks to Lourdes Portillo and Corey Sabourin. This cinematic renaissance in Latin American has coincided with the emergence of left-leaning governments, as well as the empowerment of the local civil society.

2. 1958 was the previous record-holding year of production in Mexican cinema with 135 titles. See John Hopewell, "Guadalajara: Mexico's Film Industry Analyzes 2016 Records, Big Picture Challenge,." *Variety*, March 15, 2017. http://variety.com/2017/film/festivals/overview-of-mexican-film-industry-2016-results-1202009705/

3. See Jeremy Kay, "Argentinian box office drew 50.5 m admissions in 2016," *Screen Daily*, January 10, 2017. http://www.screendaily.com/box-office/argentinian-box-office-drew-505m-admissions-in-2016/5112675.article

4. See Martin Dale, "Central America Records 'Unbelievable' Box-Office Surge in 2015," *Variety*, April 8, 2016. http://variety.com/2016/film/global/central-america-records-unbelievable-box-office-surge-2015-1201748536/.

5. See Jeremy Kay, "Colombian box office hits record heights in 2016," *Screen Daily*, January 30, 2017. http://www.screendaily.com/box-office/colombian-box-office-hits-record-heights-in-2016/5114343.article.

6. See John Hecht and Agustín Mango, "Why Latin America's Film Market Has Never Been Hotter," *The Hollywood Reporter*, February 13, 2017. http://www.hollywoodreporter.com/lists/why-latin-americas-film-market-has-never-been-hotter-975368.

7. Director Lucrecia Martel talks about her fellow Argentinean filmmakers of her generation: "We know each other, we greet each other cordially, but I couldn't really say that I can count them among my friends." See Academy Visual History with Lucrecia Martel, interviewed by Lourdes Portillo in Hollywood, October 3, 2014, Academy of Motion Picture Arts and Sciences, October 5, 2014.

8. In 2010, Cinema Tropical did a survey of the best Latin American films of the decade among film professionals based in New York City, and the three films by Lucrecia Martel landed in the top ten, and *La ciénaga* was named the Best Latin American Film of the Aughts.

9. "I was in my senior year at college, but I loved my job so much and I had been given so many responsibilities that when I went to classes at the university I was bored with my professors, I wasn't learning anything, so I decided not to graduate. It did not make any sense to me." Academy Visual History with Alejandro G. Iñárritu, interviewed by Lourdes Portillo, Academy of Motion Picture Arts and Sciences, September 2, 2016.

10. See Iñárritu.

11. Cuarón describes how he fell into a depression after one film in Hollywood that he didn't really believe in after an undisclosed production company canceled a film project that he had written and was to direct with a cast and locations in place. "I went into a depression, rather, to a total disenchantment of the cinema, I did not like the cinema, I did not like the cinema people, I did not like anything." "Academy Visual History with Alfonso Cuarón, interviewed by Lourdes Portillo, Academy of Motion Picture Arts and Sciences, February 11, 2016.

12. At Sundance, three Chilean films have won the World Cinema Dramatic Jury Prize in a period of six years: Sebastián Silva's *The Maid* (*La nana*) in 2009, Andrés Wood's *Violeta Went to Heaven* (*Violeta se fue a los cielos*) in 2012, and Alejandro Fernández Almendras's *To Kill a Man* (*Matar a un hombre*) in 2014. In 2012 Chile received its first Oscar nomination by the hand of Pablo Larraín's *No*, starring the Mexican actor Gael García Bernal.

13. Peruvian filmmaker Claudia Llosa won the Golden Bear at the Berlinale for her film *The Milk of Sorrow* (*La teta asustada*, 2009), which became the first film from Peru to ever receive an Oscar nomination for Best Foreign Language Film.

14. *Embrace of the Serpent* (*El abrazo de la serpiente*, Ciro Guerra, 2015) won the top prize at the Directors' Fortnight section of the Cannes Film Festival, giving Colombia its first Academy Award nomination, and becoming an international sensation. In the U.S. it grossed the considerable amount of $1.3 million at the box office.

15. Such as Juan Manuel Echevarría and Carlos Motta from Colombia, Beatriz Santiago Muñoz from Puerto Rico, Vik Muniz from Brazil, Adrián Villar Rojas from Argentina, and Miguel Calderón and Artemio from Mexico, just to name a few.

16. The term "Third Cinema" was coined by Argentinean directors Fernando Solanas and Octavio Getino, who defined it as "the cinema that recognizes in (the anti-imperialist struggle in the Third World and its equivalents within the imperialist countries) . . . the most gigantic cultural, scientific, and artistic manifestation of our time . . . in a word, the decolonization of culture" (Solanas and Getino quoted in In Ella Shohat and Robert Stam, *Unthinking Eurocentrism: Multiculturalism and the Media* (London, England: Routledge, 1994), 28.

17. See Martel.

18. See Martel.

19. Cuarón says that he wasn't interested at first in directing the film for the Harry Potter franchise. He describes how his friend, director Guillermo del Toro, convinced him to take the job. See Cuarón.

20. "I can live abroad, but my head always thinks about Mexico and as a Mexican I am always aware of what is happening in my country . . . returning to Mexico to make movies was a necessity," Alfonso Cuarón quoted in Zack Sharf, "Alfonso Cuarón is Done Filming 'Roma,' Says It's The Movie He 'Always Dreamed of' Making," *IndieWire*, March 14, 2017.

21. In a controversial comment made at a public conference in Mexico, and later reported by the press, Cannes artistic director Thierry Frémaux reportedly said that "after an important moment we expected more, but it never grew, Argentine filmmakers committed suicide." Frémaux quoted in Marcelo Stiletano, "Frémaux, en el ojo de la tormenta," *La Nación*, March 3, 2012. http://www.lanacion.com.ar/1453300-fremaux-en-el-ojo-de-la-tormenta

22. See Iñárritu.

Far Left: Poster for *Nostalgia for the Light*. A film by Patricio Guzmán. Poster courtesy Icarus Films.

Center Left: Poster for *La teta asustada* (*Milk of Sorrow*, Claudia Llosa, 2009).

INDEX

PHOTO CREDITS

Cast and crew portrait, *The Cat Creeps*, 1930. Courtesy Universal Studios. All Rights Reserved.

Cimarron, 1931 Courtesy Turner Entertainment Company. All Rights Reserved.

Ben-Hur poster painting, 1925. Courtesy of the Academy's Margaret Herrick Library.

Ben-Hur costume drawing, 1925. Courtesy Turner Entertainment Company. All Rights Reserved.

Antonio Moreno in *The Bad Man*, 1931. Courtesy Turner Entertainment Company. All Rights Reserved.

Lupe Vélez in *Mexican Spitfire*. Courtesy Turner Entertainment Company. All Rights Reserved.

Carlos Villar and Carmen Guerrero in *Drácula*, 1931. Courtesy Universal Studios. All Rights Reserved.

Lupita Tovar, ca. 1931. Courtesy Universal Studios. All Rights Reserved.

Santa poster, 1932. Courtesy Televisa Foundation. All Rights Reserved.

Jorge Ruiz on set, 1958. Courtesy Jorge Ruiz.

Jorge Sanjinés, 1985. Coutesy José Sánchez-H.

Tomás Gutíerrez Alea meeting Che Guevara. Courtesy Getty Images.

Nelson Pereira dos Santos on set of *How Tasty Was My Little Frenchman*, 1971. Courtesy Nelson Pereira dos Santos.

The Clandestine Nation, 1989. Courtesy Grupo Ukamau.

Luís Valdez, 1966. Getty Images/ Gerald French.

Zoot Suit, 1981. Courtesy Universal City Pictures, Inc. All Rights Reserved.

The Ballad of Gregorio Cortez, 1982. Courtesy Canal+. All Rights Reserved.

El Norte. Courtesy Gregory Nava.

Gregory Nava in Mexico. Courtesy of Gregory Nava.

Courage of the People, 1971. Courtesy Grupo Ukamau.

Motorcycle Diaries, 2004. Courtesy Focus Features and FilmFour Ltd.

Embrace of the Serpent, 2015. Photo courtesy of Oscilloscope Laboratories.

Luís Valdez on the set of *La Bamba*, 1987. Courtesy Columbia Pictures. All Rights Reserved.

Gregory Nava and others on the set. Courtesy Gregory Nava.

Portrait of Edward James Olmos. Courtesy Dana Fineman.

My Family, 1995. Courtesy New Line Pictures. All Rights Reserved.

Blade Runner, 1982. Courtesy Warner Bros. Entertainment. All Rights Reserved.

American Me costume design drawing. Courtesy Universal City Studios, Inc. All Rights Reserved.

Stand and Deliver, 1988. Courtesy Warner Bros. Entertainment. All Rights Reserved.

Selena, 1997. Courtesy Warner Bros. Entertainment. All Rights Reserved.

María Novaro at Rome Film Festival, 2010. Courtesy Getty Images.

Danzón poster, 1991. Courtesy of María Novaro.

Lucrecia Martel on the set of *The Headless Woman*, 2008. Courtesy Strand Releasing USA.

La ciénaga, 2001. Courtesy Janus films.

Lila Stantic with Lucrecia Martel at the Cannes Film Festival, 2004. Courtesy Getty Images/Elisabetta A. Villa.

America Ferrara and Lupe Ontiveros at the Toronto Film Festival, 2002. Courtesy Getty Images.

Real Women Have Curves poster, 2002. Courtesy Getty Images.

The Devil Never Sleeps poster, 1994. Courtesy Lourdes Portillo.

Missing Young Woman, 2001. Courtesy Lourdes Portillo.

Pan's Labyrinth poster, 2006. Courtesy Warner Bros. Entertainment. All Rights Reserved.

Alicia Paz Garcíadiego with Arturo Ripstein at *La calle de la amargura* premiere, 72nd Venice Film Festival. Courtesy Getty Images/ Tristan Fewings.

Kiss of the Spider Woman courtesy of David Weisman, © Copyright 1985, Independent Cinema Restoration Archive LLC.

Sleep Dealer screening at the 2008 Sundance Film Festival. Courtesy Getty Images/ Matthew Simmons.

Born in East LA, 1987. Courtesy Universal City Studios, Inc. All Rights Reserved.

Amores perros, 2000. Courtesy Lionsgate and Alejandro G. Iñárritu.

Nelson Pereira dos Santos with Agnes Varda, Wim Wenders, and Werner Herzog, c. 1975-1980. Courtesy Getty Images.

Edward James Olmos and Marlene Demer, 2013. Los Angeles Latino International Film Festival - Opening night Gala. Courtesy Getty Images/JC Olivera.

Real Women Have Curves Sundance Premiere, 2002. Courtesy Getty Images/Jeff Kravitz.

Lucrecia Martel at the Berlin Film Festival, 2001. Courtesy Getty Images/ Ronald Siemoneit.

Gravity, 2013. Courtesy Warner Bros. Entertainment. All Rights Reserved.

Birdman, 2014. Courtesy 20th Century Fox. All Rights Reserved.

The Revenant, 2015. Courtesy 20th Century Fox and Leonardo DiCaprio. All Rights Reserved.

Ixcanul, 2015. Courtesy Kino Lorber.

La Libertad, 2001. Courtesy Lisandro Alonso.

City of God, 2002. Courtesy Miramax and O2 Filmes. All Rights Reserved.

Miracles from Heaven, 2016. Courtesy Columbia Pictures. All Rights Reserved.

Milk of Sorrow, 2009. Courtesy Olive Filmes.

The Constant Gardener, poster, 2005. Courtesy Universal City Studios, Inc. All Rights Reserved.

Nostalgia for the Light. A film by Patricio Guzmán. Poster courtesy Icarus Films.

FOREWORD BY
SANDRA CISNEROS

Sandra Cisneros is a poet, short story writer, novelist, essayist, whose work explores the lives of the working-class. Her numerous awards include *NEA fellowships* in both poetry and fiction, the *Texas Medal of the Arts*, a *MacArthur* Fellowship, several honorary doctorates and book awards nationally and internationally, and most recently Chicago's *Fifth Star Award*, the *PEN Center USA Literary Award* and the *National Medal of the Arts*, awarded to her by President Obama in 2016. *The House on Mango Street* has sold over five million copies, been translated into over twenty languages, and is required reading in elementary, high school, and universities across the nation. Founder of awards and foundations that serve writers and a dual citizen of the United States and Mexico, Sandra Cisneros earns her living by her pen.

Library of Congress Cataloguing-in-Publication Data

From Latin America to Hollywood: Latino Film Culture in Los Angeles 1967-2017/
text by Cari Beauchamp, Catherine L. Benamou, Carlos E. Cortés, Rosa-Linda Fregoso,
Carlos A. Gutiérrez, José Sánchez-H., Laura Isabel Serna; foreword by Sandra Cisneros;
edited by Lourdes Portillo and Ellen M. Harrington.
Includes Index.
ISBN 978-0-692-91132-7
Library of Congress Control Number: 2017949009
1. Latin American Filmmakers. 2. Motion Picture History. 3. Latino and Chicano Film Studies

ACKNOWLEDGMENTS

The Academy of Motion Picture Arts and Sciences'
Pacific Standard Time: LA/LA Project wishes to thank:

Advisory Committee: Cari Beauchamp, Catherine L. Benamou,
Carlos E. Cortés, Rosa-Linda Fregoso, Carlos A. Gutiérrez, José Sánchez-H.,
Laura Isabel Serna

Guest Curator: Lourdes Portillo
Curator: Ellen M. Harrington

Chief Executive Officer: Dawn Hudson
Managing Director, Preservation and Foundation Programs: Randy Haberkamp
Director, Margaret Herrick Library: Linda Harris Mehr
Director, Academy Film Archive: Michael Pogorzelski

Creative Director: Ford Oelman
Book Design: Nicholas Banos
Art Production Supervisor: Amanda Tannen
Project Management: Drayton Benedict
Copy Editors: Linda Hart, Amy Dunkleberger

Coordinator, Planning Phase: Dara Jaffe
Editorial Assistants, Graduate Interns: Sophia Serrano Wagner, Jennifer Alpert
Research: Raul Guzman
Clearances: Kristen Ray
Margaret Herrick Library Graphic Arts & Photography Departments:
Anne Coco, Matt Severson, Jeanie Braun, Elizabeth Cathcart, Michael Hartig

Oral History Project: Teague Schneiter, Mae Woods, Jade Takahashi, Genevieve
Maxwell
Directors of Photography: PJ Gaynard, Jonathan Harris, Daniel Jaroschik,
Heloisa Passos, Santiago Torres, Chad Wilson
Editors: Caitlin Díaz, Eliane Lima, Carolina Charry Quintero, Josiah Patrow